STAYING AFTER SCHOOL

At-Risk Students in a Compensatory Education Program

Bram A. Hamovitch

 PRAEGER

Westport, Connecticut
London

Library of Congress Cataloging-in-Publication Data

Hamovitch, Bram A., 1949–
    Staying after school : at-risk students in a compensatory
education program / Bram A. Hamovitch.
        p.   cm.
    Includes bibliographical references and index.
    ISBN 0–275–95701–2 (alk. paper)
    1. Compensatory education—United States.   2. Socially handicapped
children—Education—United States.   I. Title.
    LC213.2.H35   1997
    370.111′0973—dc20   96–36368

British Library Cataloguing in Publication Data is available.

Library of Congress Catalog Card Number: 96–36368
ISBN: 0–275–95701–2

First published in 1997

Praeger Publishers, 88 Post Road West, Westport, CT 06881
An imprint of Greenwood Publishing Group, Inc.

Printed in the United States of America

The paper used in this book complies with the
Permanent Paper Standard issued by the National
Information Standards Organization (Z39.48–1984).

10 9 8 7 6 5 4 3 2 1

Contents

Acknowledgments

The completion of this book involved the assistance and support of many people. First, it should be acknowledged that OSRP students and staff were invaluable in helping me to understand themselves and their program. Without their openness, I could never have written this book. I would also like to acknowlege the support of Robert Stevenson, Catherine Cornbleth, Mwalimu Shujaa, and Michael Sedlak. Each of these individuals read and commented on the text in different (and yet helpful) ways. Last, I would like to express my gratitude to my wife and good friend, Terry, who patiently read and commented on this project more times than I can count.

1

Introduction: At-Risk Students, Schools and Compensatory Education Programs

In the years since the early 1960s, there has been an explosion in the number and types of programs that try to assist students who are having difficulty in schools, or who are labeled as being at risk of having difficulty in the future. These compensatory education programs seek to remedy a problem or deficit that identified students are thought to have. It appears that the public supports these measures, as they are allocated relatively significant government resources. Yet, how much is really known about the operation of these programs?

This book explores a career-oriented compensatory education program that is designed to identify and then help to reintegrate poor, alienated high school students into their schools. I call it OSRP (Ordered School Reinforcement Program). As the staff see it, the program attempts to introduce order into the sometimes chaotic lives of the participating students. OSRP reinforces the schools in the sense that its main purpose is to convince its students to successfully reintegrate into their schools. Using ethnographic methods, I immersed myself in the activities of OSRP between January and July 1992.[1] I found that most OSRP staff, students, and parents were not aware of the fact that the program failed to accomplish its main goal, successful school reintegration. I ask here why it failed, how it is that participants could be unaware of its failure, and what other avenues exist to address the equity issues raised by the perceived need for the program.

Problems commonly related to poor school performance include poverty, hunger, having a "deficient" family life, having a first language other than English, having a learning disability, being alienated from school, and exhibiting behavior problems in school. Compensatory education programs include, among others: school breakfast and lunch programs, Head Start, Follow Through, Title I remedial reading and math programs, peer tutoring, bilingual education programs, after-school job-related programs, desegregation programs, learning centers, special education programs, and grants for school districts having high concentrations of poor children.

There are several ways of looking at compensatory education. The most widely accepted view is that remedial programs help to "level the playing field" (Ramey and Johnson, 1991; Ramey, 1992; U.S. Department of Education, 1993). This perspective suggests that we can identify children who suffer from deficits that put them at a disadvantage in schools. It is argued that members of the identified groups (e.g., the poor or minorities) can and do benefit from programs that compensate for their deficiencies. In principle, the problem is remedied, and the student is then successfully reintegrated into mainstream classes, where he orshe should be able to compete with other students.

Some critics of compensatory education agree with the philosophy of these programs, but have concerns about their implementation (e.g., Gabriel and Rasp, 1986). These observers argue that the programs fail to reach all or even most of those students who qualify for them. Others contend that even when remedial programs do reach those in need, they are often ineffective because they tend to lack adequate funding and staffing (e.g., Reyes, 1995).

A third perspective is held among critical educators who argue that compensatory programs divert attention from the real problems of schooling (Carnoy, 1975; Cummins, 1986; Frost, 1994; O'Brien, 1993). Gartner and Riessman comment that helping often benefits the helper more than it does the object of help because these relations tend to be asymmetrical, inviting the passivity of the helped (1993, 1994). It appears that two of the major results of remedial education are to label poor students and to segregate them from those who are achieving normally. Since compensatory education is a broadly accepted policy of governments and school administrators, this suggests that officials may be seen as working in the interests of good learners by separating them from potential distractions. In the view of these critics, compensatory education programs operate by "blaming the victims." In negatively labeling participants of such programs, they reinforce notions of difference or inferiority. Furthermore, these programs divert attention from wider issues. From a critical perspective, inflexible curricula, poor relationships between teachers and students, and the organization of schools (including their tendency to silence student voice and their competitive nature) create a climate in which it is inevitable that some students fail to thrive (Anyon, 1995; Fine, 1987). Hence, these critics conclude that the problem lies with our schools, rather than with those who fail to succeed within them. Schools will continue to reproduce power relations in the wider community until organizational and interaction patterns are changed within them.

The position adopted here most closely approximates this third perspective. In part, this reflects my personal attachment to a preferred paradigm. In addition, it is a response to what was found in the data gathered for this study. These findings most clearly support the basic suppositions found within critical theory, despite efforts to test alternative interpretations. Before discussing this theoretical perspective in more detail, it is important to understand how students who are prime candidates for compensatory education programs relate to their schools. In a word, many at-risk students find themselves "alienated" from school. Researchers have asked about the causes of this alienation.

ALIENATION FROM SCHOOL

There is voluminous literature on the alienation from school experienced by many high school students. These studies help us understand what factors might be associated with the reality that many young people fail to engage themselves successfully with their school work, thus making some of them candidates for compensatory programs. They also anticipate the school context as the students in this study experience it, both while they are in the compensatory program and, later, without its support.

It is useful to distinguish between factors external to schools that affect the likelihood that students will integrate successfully and those that act within schools to accomplish the same result. Many studies find that alienation from school emanates from students' social class (Anyon, 1981; Bernstein, 1977; Bourdieu, 1977; Bowles and Gintis, 1976; Tripp, 1986; Woods, 1990). Schools are seen as reproducing social class distinctions by presenting different programs to different groups and by differentiating among students with varying states of preparedness, both of which are related to social class. Students' racial characteristics have also been found to alter their experience of school, in that there tends to be a cultural schism between schools and nonwhite students (Fordham, 1991; Ogbu, 1974, 1978; Weis, 1985). Race, like class, is thought of as baggage that students, teachers, and administrators carry with them to the school site. Because these factors influence the lived experience of students, race and class affect their relationship with schools.

In addition, researchers have found that schools themselves create conditions leading to student differentiation. Implicit understandings of how things ought to be done promote student differentiation and alienation. Studies have examined, for example, tracking, the teacher role, teaching methods, curriculum knowledge, the internal organization of the school, and the policies and practices of the school bearing directly on the issue of racial stratification. I shall consider each of these briefly in turn.

The literature on tracking argues that curriculum grouping plays a significant role in the differentiation process (Coleman et al., 1966; Jencks et al., 1972; Oakes, 1985; Rosenbaum, 1976; Rutter et al., 1979; Sedlak et al., 1986). There is a relationship between the social class of students and their track placement (Woods, 1990). The experience of school differs noticeably according to track placement—that is, lower track students tend to get a watered down academic curriculum and the "leftover" teachers who are not considered to be the most experienced or respected (Fensham, 1986).

High school teachers feel constrained within their role, and want to be instructors of curriculum first and foremost (Goodlad, 1984; Powell et al., 1985; Sizer, 1984). Teachers tend to psychologize their relations with their students: they explain and excuse student behavior in relation to real or imagined therapeutic or family problems. Their role does not allow them to respond to the ordinary human needs of individuals who have problems adapting to their role as student. Thus, because school contexts encourage teachers to maintain a distant relationship with students, label them, and blame them for their inadequacies, schools contribute to the process of student differentiation.

Researchers exploring teaching methods used in high schools have produced consistent findings on alienation. Cusick's (1973) study of working-class senior high school students revealed that teachers do nearly all the acting (talking) within the typical lesson. Similarly, Wehlage et al.'s (1989) examination of ten programs for at-risk students found that students were, more often than not, mere spectators in their own education. Like Goodlad (1984), Wehlage et al. noted that the words "watch" and "wait" describe much of the student activity in the classroom. Sizer's (1984) study of Horace's school yielded similar findings. He concluded that teachers "anaesthetize" their students through a lack of stimulus or intellectual challenge. The result is that students interact poorly with the curriculum—they have a series of meaningless encounters with learning. Since boredom with an uninspired curriculum is a problem shared by the majority of high school students, it is not surprising that segments of the student population are alienated enough from the process to drop out or behave unacceptably.

Ginsburg (1988) and Cornbleth (1990) concur that school learning generally follows a cultural transmission model. Knowledge is presented to students as given (rather than problematical) and molecular (not holistic), while personal knowledge is underutilized (in comparison to public knowledge). In general, classrooms are seen as relatively sterile places that do not encourage students to engage all of their selves in the process. Empirical studies of high schools have largely confirmed these theoretical analyses (Everhart, 1983; Fensham, 1986; Goodlad, 1984; Tripp, 1986). Fensham argues that relevance within the classroom is likely to remain an illusive goal. He feels that many students now reject school knowledge just because of the context in which it is taught. According to Everhart, the hidden information that most students receive from their schools is that they are not fit to exercise power because of their personal limitations. Only a small minority of students receive the opposite message.

The organization of schools may also contribute to the alienation of many students. Historians such as Callahan (1962) and Tyack (1974) have documented the bureaucratization, the rationalization, the centralization of decisionmaking, the exclusion of nonelite groups from the decision-making process, and the predominance of business values within contemporary public schools. These elements are now taken for granted, yet they did not always exist within schools. Such historical trends have resulted in depersonalized schools, the disempowerment of diverse elements within communities, and the exclusion of large numbers from meaningful participation within the system. While students remain the official central concern of schools, the schools' very structure tends to objectify many students. As Hummel and Nagel argue, "the bureaucratic model is inconsistent with the kind of organizational structure required for maximum learning and creative teaching" (1975).

Wright (1986, 1987), Woods (1990), and Solomon (1989) have investigated the impact of race upon students' high school experiences. In general, they found that race acts inside the school to give groups of students systematically different experiences.   Because "whiteness" is valued relative to "blackness" in schools, African Americans often find schools to be a source of self-doubt rather than self-development (Ladson-Billings and Tate, 1995; Shujaa, 1993). This is accomplished through various forms of institutional and personal racism, including disproportionate lower track assignment, teacher racism, and a culture of sport rather than academic engagement. The concomitant patterns of displacing academic focus with socializing and of strained interracial peer relations are predictable, given this context of institutional discrimination. African American and other minority students often find themselves alienated from schools for understandable and predictable reasons that have more to do with patterns of accepted behavior within schools than with the abilities or talents of the young people themselves.

THEORETICAL ORIENTATION

A deeper discussion of external factors might suggest that society is composed of dominant and subordinate groups with different access to power and other resources. From this perspective, groups often have distinct ways of speaking, related to dissimilar experiences, values, perceptions, and economic interests. It appears that schools often embrace the culture and interests of the dominant social or economic groups, which necessarily influences the degree to which schools can adequately socialize all groups of students. For example, Bowles and Gintis (1976) see the hierarchical relationships within schools as corresponding to those found in the economy. This means that social class plays a significant part in determining how different categories of students experience school. Tyack (1974) documents the historical trend toward control of local school boards by the most privileged members of the community. The result is that schools tend to ease the success of sons and daughters of the dominant groups and impede the progress of others.

Apart from learning, schools' most salient purpose is to differentiate among their students. This aim is apparent in tracking and grading. But it is also supported by less obvious institutional arrangements, such as those that restrict caring and personal communication between teachers and students, in teacher definitions of their work and their students, and in a curriculum that is alienating. These are factors affecting all students. However, the research tends to support the conclusion that schools are experienced differently by students from subordinate groups, who often find themselves in lower tracks, getting lower grades, having access to fewer resources, and so forth. It is therefore not surprising that certain groups feel more alienated from our public schools than others. This is predominantly a matter of control: even though all taxpayers theoretically manage public education policy through their right to vote, effective power is held by dominant groups. The predictable result is inordinate alienation by students whose parents are relatively powerless: in this study, by poor and racial minority at-risk students.

The control of schools shares some of the characteristics of the street corner gang, as analyzed by W. F. Whyte (1943) in his classic ethnography. Whyte observed that the bowling scores of the gang that he studied closely approximated the system of ranking within the group itself: the top bowlers also happened to be the group's leaders. In trying to explain why this occurred, Whyte argued that bowling acted to reinforce the leaders' dominant position within the group. High bowling scores, however, did not in themselves explain the leaders' power. Whyte determined that it was the leaders themselves who chose bowling to be one of the important group activities. In making this choice, the group leaders were selecting something that was bound to reinforce their status within the group because of their own excellence at it. Presumably, if they had chosen an alternative sport or activity at which others were more skilled, it might have served to undermine their own authority. This, predictably, did not occur.

Furthermore, Whyte observed that the leaders, having secured their own advantage against their bowling opponents and social subordinates, unconsciously instituted mechanisms to ensure that the desired outcome regularly occurred. A lower status bowler who was "bowling over his head" would be ridiculed, often resulting in loss of self-confidence and a subsequent lowering of bowling scores. On the other hand, a high status player who was bowling poorly was interpreted as having bad luck or a temporary lapse. In addition, status within the group and expected bowling performance were repeatedly reinforced by the "pick-up" team selection method. This had the effect of publicly reminding everybody of their proper place within the status/bowling hierarchy, adding to the difficulty of achieving individual social mobility.

There are parallels that can be drawn between Whyte's analysis and our society at large. Like the street corner gang, our society is made up of those having and lacking resources. Despite contradictory evaluations of existing evidence, gaining and losing significant amounts of status appears to be difficult within our larger society,[2] just as it was for Whyte's gang members. This is at least partly because society (like the gang) has established "hoops" through which we all must jump to gain upward mobility. And the nature and quality of those hoops has been set to a large extent by those who have the power and means to make such decisions. Like Whyte's leaders, our society's ruling class have created institutions (e.g., schools) that reflect what they do best and that reinforce their existing status. Those who have resources can use them to control the activities that institutions endorse and reward. This has the effect of legitimating and more or less ensuring the continuation of their own dominance (and that of their children). As in the bowling example, schools have constant reminders of what is expected of low status and high status students (Rist, 1973) and use ridicule and other methods of social control to keep people in their place.

The perspective adopted here may be seen as a reaction to functionalist sociology. These researchers observe the continued presence of stratification within societies and try to explain its persistence. Functionalists implicitly or explicitly take the position that if inequalities have existed since the dawn of recorded history, there must be functional reasons for this. Researchers working within this paradigm have an organic view of society (Nisbet, 1952). They imagine that societies are like organisms, having various parts that each make their own unique contribution to the functioning of the whole. According to Nisbet, they are part of a conservative tradition within sociology that fears that the elimination of hierarchy would lead to the obliteration of the natural channels of transmission of cultural values. Parsons is the most famous modern-day theorist within this tradition. His theory of social stratification (1954) legitimates the continued existence of structured inequalities within society by theorizing their relationship to an omnipresent central value system. According to this theory, some work roles better represent our society's valuation of efficiency. At the same time, some individuals possess more of the qualities that society values than others. We pay the most valued job incumbents well in order to attract the most competent into those positions. Since these individuals gain the highly desired jobs, we end up with a system of inequality that is basically functional and fair. This is the academic version of the mainstream view of our system of social stratification that I will later refer to as the "conservative ideology of hope."

As suggested above, the orientation that I carry into this research draws heavily on critical theory. According to Gibson (1986), critical theory can be understood by its concern about inequalities: its mission is to trace their origins and to suggest remedies. Critical theory rejects the liberal notion that education is an inherent good that could eventually eradicate inequalities within society. Instead, it posits that education tends to reproduce preexisting economic relationships (Bowles and Gintis, 1976). It views schools as serving state ends, reproducing the power and ideology of the state by socializing workers to support existing economic and political structures (Althusser, 1972). Schools are viewed as reproducing inequality by their choice of cultural expression and transmission that systematically excludes and disadvantages some groups (Bernstein, 1977; Bourdieu, 1977). It seeks to identify subgroups where resistance and conflict currently exist or might develop to emancipate people from the above patterns of social control (Willis, 1977; Apple, 1976). Inherent in this last perception is the understanding that humans are never completely socialized by socializing agencies, that they can and do create (as well as sometimes passively accept) social institutions, and that they strive for individual autonomy (as well as group acceptance).

My theoretical predispositions are interpretive as well as critical. This means that I have a particular interest in how actors comprehend their personal and institutional contexts. I do not accept as given that individuals understand their world in a rational manner that is consistent with my own or anyone else's ideas. Institutional definitions and demands are not passively incorporated into the subjective consciousness of role players. Rather, I see group and individual interpretations as mediating between institutions and individual behaviors. I am interested in seeing the relationship between actions and the ideas people attach to those actions. Important questions include: How do the meanings that people attach to their actions help to determine their relationship to institutions? Is there a consistency between understandings and actions? In short, my predisposition is to accept W. I. Thomas's dictum that one's "definition of the situation" is of key importance in understanding social behavior (Hollander and Hunt, 1967). Categories of analysis should emerge from the experiences and perceptions of one's subjects, as opposed to the research literature. The perspectives of others should be a matter for investigation: as few assumptions should be made about their nature and quality as possible.

From either a critical or a functionalist perspective, compensatory education may be seen as an extension of compulsory schooling; both often attempt to integrate students who have not yet been successfully socialized into the dominant society. Critical theorists argue that both regular and compensatory schooling involve an investment of resources by the ruling class in an attempt to shape the outlook of subordinate groups, making them generally supportive of the existing system (Gouldner, 1976). Within schools and compensatory programs, a network of ideas helps to strengthen the adhesion of the nonruling class to the interests of the ruling class. This set of ideas constitutes ideology, in Gouldner's analysis. What the ruling class seeks is a society in which the masses are sympathetic to their (ruling class) problems. This can be achieved by encouraging "the other classes [to] define the social world in ways congenial to its own concerns and interests, and supportive of the interlocking institutions within which they exist, and whose normal functioning reproduces the hegemonic class" (p. 233). Thus, the ruling class seeks loyalty to the system, as opposed to personal or class loyalty.

Like religion, Gouldner sees ideology as attempting to shape people's behaviors. Unlike religion, however, ideologies tend to focus on behaviors that are political in nature. They are networks of ideas that become part of culture, structuring the roles people can play and the types of persons we become. Ideologies simplify a complex reality, helping us to define and interpret social situations. At the same time, they suggest to people that they possess power to overcome obstacles or change the world. The people, far from being downtrodden or enslaved, are characterized in both conservative and radical ideologies as being the source of power. Thus, ideologies might be expected to produce feelings of self-worth and self-confidence.

The writings of Paulo Freire, who participated in and studied agricultural and literacy programs in Brazil and Chile, anticipate many of the findings of this study of a compensatory education program. Freire discusses relationships between teachers/agronomists and peasants/students (1970, 1973). He notes that they are typically characterized by the teacher's attitude of superiority over students. From the educator's perspective, he or she must try to persuade the peasant to follow the precepts of modern agricultural technique. The accepted image is that of the educator attempting to socialize, delivering content partially in the form of propaganda, to the ignorant student. Knowledge is treated as though it is something static and absolute to be deposited in the minds of students. Predictably, students often respond to this form of education with docility and passivity, that is, by resisting their treatment as objects.

Given this typical student response, Freire argues that the usual form of presenting knowledge is doomed to failure. Knowledge is located within a nexus of meaning that we call "culture." Presenting one's own knowledge as absolute is a form of cultural invasion because it denies the validity of the student's own ways of knowing. (Even the magic of many South American peasants has an integrity and logic that is based on their own culture and praxis.) The solution to reaching students of a different culture involves rethinking the concept of knowledge as something dynamic. Knowledge presupposes a searching curiosity about the world, requiring "transform-ing action on reality" (Freire, 1973, p. 101). To Freire, the successful teacher must abandon the self-image of being all-knowing, with a corresponding conception of students as needing to be filled up with the teacher's knowledge. Instead, it is the role of the teacher to make the accepted world of the students more problematic, and to engage in dialogue with them. This involves an openness to the students' culture and ways of understanding, rather than attempts to superimpose one's own culture over theirs.

The term "cultural invasion" was used above to describe the typical relationship that Freire observed between teachers/agronomists and peasants/students. These relationships are ones of authority, in which the teacher/invader acts, while the students absorb, having had another do their thinking for them: "The invader thinks, at most, *about* the invaded, never *with* them; the latter have their thinking done for them by the former. The invader dictates; the invaded patiently accept what is dictated" (Freire, 1973, p. 113.) Thus, cultural invasion entails manipulation on the part of the invader to achieve certain objectives. This is usually accomplished with the assistance of propaganda, slogans, and myths (rather than dialogue). The procedure is often justified on the basis that there is no time for dialogue, since the curriculum is so full of things to be urgently learned. The notion that students might have good decision-making abilities is implicitly denied.

Freire argues that this form of education is founded on an unjustified lack of faith in students, incorrectly assuming their ignorance and passivity. The absence of dialogue reflects the teacher's underestimation of the students' powers of reflection and of their ability to seek knowledge. Freire cites the social distance (social class difference) separating the teacher and the student as a factor contributing to the problems of true communication between them. People have been conditioned to recognize the importance of status differences between themselves and others, and these have implications for education. The peasants have learned a "consciousness of the oppressed" and have little experience of near-equal dialogue or participation with higher status individuals. As a consequence, they are often unsure of themselves in such interactions. When students fail to achieve teachers' desired outcomes, teachers have a tendency to explain that failure as being related to the natural incapacity of the peasants.

From Freire's perspective, then, the lack of dialogue between educator and student is not an individual problem, but results from the hierarchical, permanent, and oppressive character of wider social structures. Freire's solution is to involve students in thinking and acting upon that wider society. Student perceptions can and will change when students are invited to rethink their reality, act upon it, and then reflect on that action. This occurs best when the educator, rather than issuing communiques, is involved with the students, entering into a process of communication with them, as a subject with other subjects. In this relationship, there are no passive parties. Rather, there is verbal communication that is meaningful to the other within his or her own frame of reference. They are subjects in search of knowing—thinking cooperatively to transform the structures that reify and oppress. This is neither a naive optimism nor a despair that paralyzes action and hope. Rather it is a critical hopefulness, a loving scientific humanism that rests on the belief that humans can make and remake their world around them.

OSRP: COMPENSATION FOR AT-RISK STUDENTS

This study explores an after school program for at-risk youth. I have called it OSRP: Ordered School Reinforcement Program. It is located in the northeastern United States, and is fully funded by the state government. The program operates at two sites within the same county, both administered by personnel hired by the local community college. One primarily serves African American adolescents in a small northeastern city that I call River City. The other is an all-white group, located in Springfield, a suburb of that city. The River City site serves seventeen African Americans, two Hispanics, and two Caucasians. Table 1.1 shows the gender and grade composition of the two groups.

Table 1.1
Gender and school grade composition of the River City and Springfield OSRP sites, January to June 1992.

| School Grade | River City | | Springfield | | Total |
	Boys	Girls	Boys	Girls	
8	4	1	1	1	7
9	3	5	2	3	13
10	2	4	1	2	9
Other[3]	1	1	1	1	4
	10	11	5	7	33

The twenty-one students at the River City location are supervised by an educator, a counselor, and by Gerald, the director. The twelve Springfield students are supervised by an educator, an aide, and a part-time counselor. While all these young people have been defined as being at risk by their schools,[4] guidance counselors regard them as "salvageable." Only regular school attenders are considered for the program, in part because students are paid the minimum hourly wage when they attend both OSRP and school on any given day.

There is nothing exceptional about the economy of these communities, when compared with that of the region and the state as a whole. The relative affluence of the two communities can be summarized by the fact that the median value of homes is fifty-one percent higher in Springfield than in River City. Like many urban areas in the United States, River City has experienced the flight of the affluent toward the suburbs. Springfield is typical of many suburbs in its relative affluence and in the newness of its buildings. It is, however, properly understood as a working-class rather than a professional suburb. Springfield is an all white community, with African

Americans comprising only 0.1 percent of its population. By contrast, 13.9 percent of River City's population is African American. Hispanics have a negligible presence in both communities.

The thirty-three students at the program's two sites are between fourteen and seventeen years of age, with twenty-nine being fifteen or sixteen years old. The students must meet financial guidelines in order to qualify for the program: they are all located below the official poverty line, with twnety-nine of the thirty-three families receiving welfare or public assistance. Eighteen of these children live with single-parent mothers, seven come from homes with a father and a mother present, four live with their mother and a step-father, two are in the care of legal guardians, one is living with her grandmother, and another is living with his father (until his mother gets out of jail).

I use the term "state" in this study to denote the state government. The concept "state," however, also has Marxist and other connotations. Structuralists employ it to suggest that the state "furthers the interests of capital or the capitalist class even though the state has relative autonomy" (Abercrombie, Hill, and Turner, 1984, p. 242). Although my contact with the state government was mostly limited to the perusal of its documents, there is some evidence of motivations deeper than simple benevolence. For example, state funding to the program had been increased on two separate occasions coincident with large-scale civil disturbances within the United States. Clearly, this evidence is not sufficient to demonstrate that the program's conception or purpose is to quell potentially troublemsome youth. In using the term "state," however, I do imply that such a possibility exists, has been considered by the author, and may also be contemplated by the reader.

The State Education Department oversees the administration of the program, setting curriculum and other guidelines that seek to ensure quality and effectiveness. According to curriculum documents, the main goal of the program is to provide economically disadvantaged at-risk students with career-oriented activities. The program attempts to show students the relationship between education and careers, tries to develop skills related to occupational success, and encourages the development of vocational goals. It provides opportunities for on-the-job experience, counseling (both personal and group), the development of life skills (i.e., communication, problem solving and decision making) and basic skills (reading, writing, speaking, and mathematics). In short, OSRP recognizes and attempts to ameliorate two related problems: high dropout rates and the cycle of poverty.

Compensatory education programs have become a fact of life in virtually all public school districts, and involve large numbers of students. Yet, how much is known about them, aside from their stated goals and the periodic assessments completed by school districts or outside agencies? Proponents applaud them because they agree with their goals. But can we safely assume that even well-rated programs succeed in their declared mission? Are they the "opportunity" they represent themselves to be?

As this study of one compensatory program will show, the outcomes of even a well-rated program fell considerably short of its stated goals. Interestingly, the degree of program failure (in its own terms) was not consciously recognized by any of its staff, nor by those within the community observing it. The program may not have been perfect in their view, but they rarely questioned its effectiveness. The staff saw themselves as participants in an ongoing program, not as critics. Casual observers were generally glad to accept program goals and functioning at face value. A typical reaction went something like this, "Isn't it nice that they're helping those poor, disadvantaged youngsters?" Annual reviews of the program were conducted by a private research firm hired by the state and by the funding department itself. Both evaluations only served to reinforce the public perception of program accomplishment.   Not long into my research, however, I came to feel that the program was unlikely to accomplish its stated objectives. Why my findings are different from the state evaluations is difficult to know with certainty. Clearly, my research methods varied from those of the other evaluators. In addition, I asked different questions, and looked for answers in different places. Perhaps it is a question of paradigm, and follows from viewing institutions from a critical perspective. At any rate, my conclusions are at odds with the official view of the program.

OSRP has a clear and straightforward goal: to reintegrate its students into their schools, thus enabling them to pursue elevated career aspirations. The staff approach this task with energy and commitment, yet with little understanding of schooling as depicted in the educational literature discussed above. The result is that criticism is purposefully silenced within the program. In its place, young people are provided with an ideology that simplifies and distorts. OSRP students feel alienated from their schools, yet lack a language of critique. The program does not assist young people to organize or articulate their feelings in a full and meaningful way.

Ideas are important because they have the power to shape people's actions. This notion is implicitly recognized by the OSRP staff, who are attempting to shape the future behavior of their students. But Marx (and others influenced by him) have taught that ideas do not emerge independently of their social context: they may be affected by such factors as class interest or position in the economy. I will argue that OSRP presents an ideology to its students that is not in their best interests. It is distorted by class and personal experience, and by an unrealistic language of hope. Because of this distortion, the language is inappropriate for the young people whom the program staff are sincerely trying to assist. The result is failure: a program that cannot deliver on its promise of individual upward mobility.

This program may reflect the way that schools in general react to their at-risk or alienated students.   Like OSRP, schools are largely staffed by middle-class professionals who share an ideological perspective that is uncritical of existing institutions (Lortie, 1975). Large numbers of teachers have experienced upward mobility, and are likely to accept the view that they have "made it" by working hard and by taking advantage of opportunities. Since society does not readily provide more complex or critical understandings of why some children fail to thrive in school, school staff (like OSRP staff) can be expected to present a simplified ideology as reality to the students.

Subsequent chapters offer more exposition and analysis. The ethnographic chapters (chapters 2 to 6) contain a mixture of data and analysis. Whenever possible, I endeavor to separate the two, allowing this distinction to remain clear to the reader. Chapter 2 examines the goals and daily routines of OSRP, exploring its failure to accomplish its own aims. Chapter 3 considers the ideology that gives the program direction and purpose. It analyzes the relationship of the students and staff to that ideology, including a discussion of the factors that seem to bind them to it. Chapters 4 to 6 focus on some of the important repercussions of this ideological restriction. Chapter 4 discusses the relationship of the staff and students to each other and to OSRP. The accepted ideology of the program sets a framework within which the staff and the students understand the roles that they are playing. This ideology limits these roles; staff do not feel free, for example, to permit criticism of institutions (such as schools) by their students. Chapter 5 highlights how the staff judge parents as blameworthy, thereby allowing themselves to act as substitute parents, with numerous repercussions. Chapter 6 presents the divergent views of OSRP staff, students, and their parents on the degree to which schools are meeting their responsibilities to these students. Despite their differences, all parties are influenced to some degree by the dominant American ideology of individual opportunity.

Finally, chapter 7 concludes with a discussion of how these findings relate to the existing literature on compensatory programs and alienated students. It also considers the implications of these findings for educators. Ultimately, the question to be discussed is how educators can best respond to the interests of the poor, the disenfranchised, and the at-risk children who inhabit our schools and our communities.

NOTES

1. For a more complete discussion of the methodology and site, refer to the Appendix.

2. Research on ascription versus achievement, the degree of openness of our society, and mobility rates reveals no consensus on whether there is a lot, some, too much, or too little inter- and intragenerational mobility. See, for example, Jencks, Crouse and Mueser (1983); Halsey (1977); Jencks et al. (1972); Lipset and Bendix (1966).

3. "Other" includes students who are in the eleventh and twelfth grades, as well as those in nongraded special education classes.

4. See the Appendix for information on the process of subject selection.

2

OSRP: Opportunity or Failure?

This chapter has three parts. First, I will investigate the goals of OSRP from the perspectives of the state funding agency, OSRP staff, and its students. Second, I will briefly sketch the various components of the formal curriculum, that is, the aspects of the program that are explicitly stated in documents. Finally, I will consider the success or failure of the program in relation to its own goals. This will be done in part by comparing the formal and the informal curricula, with the latter being the actual practices and experiences of the students and staff.

PROGRAM GOALS

State curriculum documents provide a formal statement of OSRP goals. They refer to the central importance of schooling to the program. OSRP students are seen as being at risk of dropping out of school, and the program is intended to be a preventative measure: "Through participation in the OSRP project, youngsters should increase their understanding of the relationship between education and a career, identify the skills needed to succeed in an occupation, increase their knowledge of a variety of potential occupations, and begin to define their personal career goals." The program only admits young people who are disadvantaged and at-risk. Students spend a year attending OSRP after school. The curriculum includes work skills, educational remediation (e.g., in literacy and numeracy), and personal and career counseling. The expected outcome of this process is improved life chances, that is, an increased likelihood of obtaining a high school diploma and going on to further education. The program aims to address the two criteria that qualify young people for entrance: their at-risk status in school and their state of poverty. The belief is that OSRP represents an opportunity that will make a difference in these children's lives.

The list of program staff in Table 2.1. may help the reader to identify the various individuals mentioned in this and subsequent discussions. The names of the persons and places have been disguised to assure the confidentiality of all subjects.

Table 2.1
OSRP staff by site location, including race and work statuses.

Stanley—full-time administrator of several welfare-related programs (Caucasian)

Gerald/Mr. Johnson—full-time OSRP director
(African American)

River City Site   **Springfield Site**

Kevin—career educator   Jane/Mrs. H.—career educator
(African American, full-time staff at a   (Caucasian, part-time substitute teacher at
River City Middle School)   Springfield High School)

Louise—counselor   Sally—counselor until pregnancy leave
(Caucasian, full-time counselor at River   (Caucasian, full-time counselor at Spring-
City High School)   field High School)

                                             Tim—counselor taking over from Sally
                                             (Caucasian, full-time counselor at Spring-
                                             field High School)

                                             Barbara—aide
                                             (Caucasian, recent college graduate)

The staff describe the program's goals in ways that are very similar to the formal state objectives outlined above. They also see OSRP as an opportunity for students to achieve success in school and in a future career. Consider what they told me in interviews about the purposes of OSRP:

Stanley: And what I'm trying to say is I think, you know, programs like OSRP are there as a beacon of hope. It's somewhere you can go and hopefully think a little bit more positive about your future. . . . If you invest hard work over the next four to eight years in your life, the likelihood is that you'll be making this kind of money and be able to afford the following kinds of things and move up the economic ladder of success and find happiness. Okay, instead of, if you sit in your neighborhood and remain on public assistance, and let everyone else determine your future for you, not so much that there's no hope, it's much more challenging as you get older.

. . .

Gerald: There's welfare mentality out there. People become dependent. And this program is trying to teach kids to be independent. . . . It's my hope that through this program, they've come to realize their potential. And persist to be something very, very prosperous down the road. At least in knowledge gained. That they feel that they have something active to contribute to society which means that they think it makes somebody want to go to college and things like this.

. . .

Jane: And basically [the state] would like to see these children who are financially eligible for this program, who have parents on welfare, they want to see these kids not follow the same welfare pattern.

The staff mentions four themes in their discussion of program goals: schooling, a future career, breaking out of the welfare cycle, and self-esteem. For them, success in school lies at the very center of OSRP because of its link to the other three factors. The program aims to help students define their career aspirations and let them experience a career directly (staff call the latter "job-trailing"). In addition, OSRP staff perceive themselves as helping to build students' self-esteem. Higher career and school aspirations are regarded as dependent on self-esteem. Staff believe that they can help young people out of their malaise or alienation from schooling. As Tim put it, career aspirations help to give students "the big picture" so they can "get some additional motivation" to succeed in school. Allison, an administrative assistant in the River City program office, summarizes the feelings that virtually all the staff share with respect to their mission in OSRP: "I would hope that the program allows for them to get that attitude, to get at least that much. They should know that they have other options. There are other avenues. They're victims of their environment. They don't have to be [poor] forever. They don't have to always be that. I think the program definitely teaches them that. Talk about being a new, improved you that's possible." As well as reiterating the official purpose, Allison's words suggest that hope is an important means to achieving OSRP aims. This word has special importance in our understanding of OSRP and its functioning, as shall be evident in subsequent chapters.

This is a well-educated and dedicated staff, who are unified in what they are trying to achieve with these young people. It is clear from observations and their words that they are serious and sincere in their work. Table 2.2 introduces the reader to all the OSRP students, prior to meeting them individually throughout the book.

When I asked OSRP students about the goals of the program, they tended to focus exclusively on career planning and schooling. They talked of career planning's role in helping them set career aspirations, giving them experience in jobs, and assisting them with skills such as doing resumés and interviews. Invariably, students turned to the importance of school, which was also emphasized in the program:

BH: Can you tell me what you think this program is all about? What is it trying to do?
Joyce: Um, teach us about the work field maybe. You know, so we learn more about jobs and real life and about college. So that we can better ourselves and try to stay in school. Because I know a lot of kids that are here [in OSRP] didn't want to stay in school. So, I don't know. Just so that they know what's out there and that they can try and everything.

. . .

Table 2.2
OSRP students by site location and gender, including age, race and job-trailing. *

	River City Site		Springfield Site
Boys:		Boys:	
Andy	15, C, clerk at pharmacy	Brian	17, C, assistant at zoo
Dewitt	15, AA, assistant to lawyer	Josh	15, C, auto parts clerk
Early	16, AA, assistant at community center	Leon	15, C, mechanic trainee
		Louis	15, C, assistant in an engineering office
Eduardo	14, H, assistant at Boys and Girls Club	Nick	17, C, printer assistant
Eric	14, AA, assistant at community center		
Hakim	16, AA, no job shadowing (Gerald: "his grades are so poor")	Girls:	
		Jen	15, C, assistant at day care center
Kente	14, AA, assistant at community center	Joyce	15, C, assistant at after school program
Lamont	16, AA, assistant at community center	Judith	15, C, florist clerk
		Nancy	15, C, assistant in a hair salon
Obuagu	16, AA, assistant at community center	Patricia	15, C, assistant in school guidance office
Wateef	14, AA, actor in play produced by Planned Parenthood	Raquel	14, C, assistant in hair salon
		Terry	14, C, student-journalist

Girls:
Argina	15, AA, assistant to OSRP secretary
Chalka	15, AA, candy striper
Davette	15, AA, assistant at Boys and Girls Club
Felicia	15, AA, candy striper
LaKesia	15, AA, candy striper
Latoya	15 AA, assistant at hair salon
Maria	15, H, assistant at school guidance office
Quionna	15, AA, data entry for university extension service
Regina	15, C, assistant at Boys and Girls Club
Shalimar	15, AA, candy striper
Yolanda	15, AA, assistant at community center

* AA denotes African American, C denotes Caucasian, and H denotes Hispanic.

BH: What's the OSR Program trying to achieve with young people?
Kente: It's trying to show them that, you know, drugs and stuff like droppin' out of school and stuff like that is a waste. Show them that you know, anybody can get an education to get anywhere in the United States.

Career planning and schooling are clearly related in the minds of these students. They understand OSRP's message that they should stay in school, think ahead to college, and use school to help them "get somewhere." These themes are similar to those voiced by the staff, but with two notable exceptions: the students are silent on the idea of breaking the cycle of poverty/welfare, and they almost never mention the goal related to self-esteem. This is understandable, since I never heard any open discussion of these ideas within the program. The staff consider these to be taboo topics, to be discussed only in confidence among themselves or with me. The result is that the students have a narrower understanding of the program than the staff: they do not realize that the program is intended to break the cycle of welfare, nor do they recognize that staff members are deliberately attempting to enhance their self-esteem.

OSRP seeks to address the problem of poverty by motivating its students to succeed in school. Staff try to accomplish this by helping the students establish career aspirations, by providing job experience, and by promoting the students' self-esteem. In the following section, I will examine how the staff take these ambitious goals and turn them into programming.

THE FORMAL CURRICULUM

This section will describe the formal curriculum as developed by the state and interpreted by the staff. Next, it will be compared with the curriculum in practice. These comparisons will help determine the degree to which OSRP succeeds or fails in its mission.

Gerald has produced a pamphlet to inform the community about program goals and activities. It is also routinely handed out to interested parents and students. After briefly quoting from that pamphlet in relation to each stated goal, I will offer some of the observations of staff, students, and myself in relation to that particular aspect of curriculum. Keep in mind that this is a formalized and idealized version of OSRP activities.

1. *Academic Remediation* [is provided] to improve [students'] skills and help them concentrate on subjects that are challenging. This is the first item mentioned in the OSRP brochure, reflecting its prominence in Gerald's eyes. The staff have told me that the first fifteen minutes to half-hour of each OSRP classroom session is set aside for completing school homework. During this time, according to the staff, students may seek individual assistance. A tutoring program was initiated by the director during the last third of the program year. It was organized in March, just in time to help students improve their grades before the final school term. Prior to its implementation, several students commented to me that they were looking forward to receiving this extra help.

2. *Career Development* [is provided] to help students make informed career choices. Students take a vocational interest survey during the first few weeks of the program. This is subsequently used to develop individual career aspirations. They then complete a library research project on five selected careers, followed by job-trailing in at least one of them (see number 4 below).

3. *Pre-Employment Skills*, including resumé writing, interviewing, and communication provide students with the necessary skills to obtain and keep a job. The activities within this category make up most of the day-to-day classroom work activities. They include thank-you letters (one from each student for each field trip or invited guest), three completed job applications, one cover letter applying for a job, letters to three colleges requesting their catalogues, a current resumé, a resumé projected forward to the year 2000, two pages of cut out "want ads" for positions related to the student's job-trailing, and a one to two page summary of each student's experiences within the program.

4. *Job-trailing* [is provided] so students can experience a career first-hand with a professional and apply their preparation to a real life situation. Several staff members told me that they consider this to be the most important part of the program, since it gives students experience in authentic work settings under the supervision of volunteers. Each student is assigned to two different settings: one chosen more or less at random during the summer, and a second (attended throughout the rest of the year) that is chosen to reflect the student's career choice. The students are paid their regular hourly wage for this time.

5. *Special Activities* such as guest speakers, field trips to colleges, work sites, and conferences provide students with exposure to educational and career choices. Field trips are sprinkled liberally throughout the program year. Staff consider the most important to be an overnight trip to a college or university. One that I attended featured meetings with representatives of career services, the admissions office, and the administration. Each student is assigned a college student host who lives at a dorm on campus. Time is allocated to allow the host and student to get to know each other casually. Gerald gives the students a "unique treat" on the return trip from the college: they are taken out for dinner in an expensive restaurant. This represents a special thank-you for being so cooperative during the field trip.

6. *Counseling* is also a part of the course of study. Students are required to undergo a minimum of two unpaid hours of group or individual counseling per month. Counseling is supposed to help students apply OSRP concepts to their own lives and cope with personal problems.

The goal of OSRP is to reverse the cycle of poverty by promoting students' self-esteem and by helping them use career aspirations and experience to motivate them to succeed in school. Career experience and pre-employment skill development are supposed to encourage career aspirations, and by extension, academic success. Tutoring and homework programs are also intended to yield school success. Counseling is thought to be linked to self-esteem, and indirectly to the elevation of career and school aspirations. Together, career aspirations, school success, and self-esteem are seen within OSRP as a partial solution to the cycle of poverty. Does this program actually achieve its stated goals? In the next section, I will consider the evidence.

OSRP'S CURRICULUM IN PRACTICE: SUCCESS OR FAILURE?

OSRP seeks to reverse the cycle of poverty by using career information/experience and emotional support to encourage long- and short-term educational success. My observations leave me in doubt, however, as to the program's ability to change the lives of its students. This conclusion is not intended as a condemnation of the program staff, for whom I have personal respect. The observations and comments of the state inspector during his annual evaluation visit testify to their hard work and ability: "I have articulated over and over that the River City/Springfield OSR Program is the model program for the state. . . . Your diligence and team work definitely paid off. . . . Congratulations for having a successful program year!" I cannot accept this evaluation (based on student testing and a one-day orchestrated visit) as being consistent with what I observed during six months of data collection. I came to understand that the program's goals would have been impossible for any staff to successfully implement, especially within the present state-mandated curriculum. Detailed discussion of why I believe the program failed follows in future chapters. My purpose here is to compare program goals with observed processes and outcomes. This section will be organized according to three of the main goals cited above—I will present each goal in relation to the evidence I was able to gather. Finally, to end the chapter, I will draw conclusions with respect to these findings.

Goal #1: Schooling

The most immediate goal of the program is to have students stay in school and succeed in the short term. Improving their academic skills (e.g., in reading and math) is expected to induce a heightened interest in school and in getting ahead. In addition, Gerald and his staff hope that increased career awareness will bring about higher aspirations and improved performance in school. Let us examine the evidence in this area.

Parents are in an excellent position to observe how well their children are doing in school, when compared with previous years. Nearly all these young people live with at least one parent; their perspective is summarized by the comments of Collena's mom.

BH: Did you see any changes in Collena this year in terms of either her schooling or her attitude toward school?

Collena's mom: Yes, beginning on like a little bit. Ya, in the beginning of the year.

BH: And what's happened since then?

CM: She just don't, like she don't care.

BH: How have her grades been this year compared to previous years?

CM: Poorly, poorly. She did poorly. This last time marking has been poor. Very poor than I ever have noticed.

OSRP parents reported a significant falling off of grades within the present school year. They do not blame OSRP for this, and they do not suggest that things might have been worse without the program.

For a more objective perspective, I consulted the grade reports of the students over the entire academic year. I looked to see if there were trends that either confirmed or contradicted the parents' perceptions. Tables 2.3 and 2.4 summarize my findings.

Table 2.3
Trends in grades in core subjects over the 1991–92 academic year (OSRP students).

Changes in Grades[1]	River City		Springfield		Total
	Boys	Girls	Boys	Girls	
Down 10+%	5	3	1	1	10 (30%)
Down 5–9.9%	1	4	1	2	8 (24%)
Down 0–4.9%	3	2	3	3	11 (33%)
Up 0–4.9%	1	2	0	1	4 (12%)
Up 5–9.9%	0	0	0	0	0 (0%)
Up 10+%	0	0	0	0	0 (0%)
	10	11	5	7	33 (99%)

Table 2.4

Average first-term grades and final term grades of students, by site and gender. *
(Note: a minimum passing grade is 65%.)

	Term 1	Final Term
River City:		
Girls	72.8% (SD=10.2)	63.5% (SD=17.2)
Boys	74.1% (SD=19.1)	60.0% (SD=19.1)
Boys & Girls	73.6% (SD=15.3)	61.3% (SD=17.7)
Springfield:		
Girls	77.8% (SD=7.9)	72.2% (SD=8.0)
Boys	69.9% (SD=12.6)	62.6% (SD=16.7)
Boys & Girls	74.8% (SD=10.3)	68.5% (SD=12.4)

* SD denotes standard deviation.

In addition to the above data, teacher comments on report cards cite lack of effort, absence from class, and behavior problems as reasons for low grades. Tables 2.3 and 2.4 support the subjective observations of the parents: most of the students' grades declined rather than increased over the course of the academic year. Why this occurred is a matter for conjecture, since this is not a trend noted among the majority of students within the schools attended by OSRP students. It appears that OSRP does not help students achieve academic success (and may even hinder them by taking up several hours a week of their time). Future chapters will explore the dynamics within the program, helping us understand why these data reveal such widespread school failure.

Finally, students spoke to me of their own perceptions of their grades this year. Joyce's remarks are representative:

BH: So you find these grades really bad?
Joyce: Considering what I was doing before. I mean, they're not really, really bad. But I know I can do better.
BH: How do you know you can do better?
Joyce: Cause I've done it before.
BH: Okay. So what's lacking now?
Joyce: I'm not, I've been slacking off. Not doing my homework, not studying for tests, everything with my friends.
BH: So you find that social life is kind of consuming you at this time of your life?
Joyce: It's very important to me. . . . I don't know. Just everything's more important. I mean, I'd rather be out with my friends than staying home doing my homework.

Almost without exception, OSRP students report that by their own standards, they are doing poorly in school, offering a variety of excuses or explanations for their poor academic achievement. (Chapter 6 will explore their relationship to their schools in detail.)

And yet OSRP staff believe that the students are in fact doing well now, in comparison with likely future performance in school. The two longest tenured staff members describe their experience with former OSRP students:

Gerald: They benefit tremendously from the program, and then most of them slip back quickly during the summer and subsequent months. In a well-funded world I would make this program more available on an as-needed [continuous] basis.

• • •

Sally: I think it's a great program, really. I would love to see it be a longer program instead of one year. . . . But once a program ends, it doesn't always carry over with these kids. And the next year, a lot of times in school, I don't know if it's a retroactive effect or what, but they got so much support in this program that now without it they flounder.

No one can tell the future. But if the observations of these staff are to be believed, schooling will continue to represent a problem to the majority of OSRP students. Despite the program's emphasis on academic achievement, it is not experiencing success in this area.

It is important to note that the two activities dealing most directly with academic remediation never really materialized within OSRP. The stated policy of homework assistance and structured homework time at the beginning of each class was simply never implemented.[2] At no point did I observe staff actively encouraging or assisting homework completion. Nor were Gerald's plans for tutoring ever realized. Rick (a tutor from the Boys and Girls club) kept hanging around once a week for a couple of months and was never assigned any tutoring by Gerald. Louise told me that Lenore (a high school teacher) was never contacted again after she had agreed to tutor students in the program. When I questioned Gerald about this, he responded that setting up a tutoring program takes more time than he has available. He added that this sort of program should properly be set up at the beginning of the year to be effective.

Thus, the two offerings most directly related to school success were never implemented. This is not to say that they would have had a significant impact on the academic results of the students. The point is that the program did not follow through in the pursuit of its main goal. Academic remediation could have created a clearer link between OSRP and school in the minds of students. As it is, they came to define the program as an after-school "job." The program wanted more, but was unable to achieve its goal.

Consider this segment from my interview with Stanley. Perhaps his attitude was responsible for the failure of the tutoring curriculum to materialize during April, May, and June:

But I think for most of them, to acquire better socialization skills, better interactive skills, better comfort levels and different environmental skills, are much much more critical for these kids to survive than getting the tutoring skills they may need to make it in school. . . . Cause generally, tutoring has an inherent misconception. The kids don't realize at first, but it's another thing you got wrong with them. And that's why, you know, sometimes I think, ya, the kids need it. But it takes them back a step or two, too. You know, the last thing you need to be telling somebody who's overweight is, "You're fat. You come to this diet workshop." They may be happy being fat. And I'm not trying to say that tutoring, if . . . their grades in school [are] to the point where they're not going to get through high school and get on to college. . . I don't think that's the case with many of our kids.

Goal #2: Career Preparation and Experience

Career preparation and experience make up four of the six OSRP curriculum objectives. This reflects the importance placed by the program and the staff on orienting students toward future careers. One important element in this process is preparing the students for work via job-trailings. According to the formal curriculum, these constitute a three-hour time commitment each week, or roughly one-third of the total program time. Two other components include classroom activities and field trips.

The picture that emerges in all three of the above areas is far from flattering to the program. I found the students' work at the job-trailing sites and within OSRP to be ritualized, trivialized, and compartmentalized. The field trips also failed to accomplish their stated purpose because the students successfully redefined their intention. Far from encouraging upward mobility, OSRP unintentionally reinforced students' place at the bottom of our system of stratification. Next, I will examine the three main parts of the career preparation program: job-trailing, classroom experience, and field trips/classroom visitors.

Job-trailing. The job-trailing aspect of OSRP offers the potential for students to experience work in a way that demands their attention and loyalty. In part, this is because they are personally involved in choosing a work site for themselves. Sometimes the supervisor at the job-trailing site knows intuitively how to relate to young people and how to involve them in a kind of work that seems "real."[3] For the placement to be successful, I found that there must be an appropriate level of challenge or demand made on the young person, accompanied by a reciprocal involvement on the part of the student.

A few of the job-trailings obviously worked well for the organization and the student. For example, Joyce told me that she came to OSRP mainly for the job-trailing. She worked at an after-school program for elementary-aged children in Springfield. Her supervisors at the program reported (and my observations confirmed) that she was able to build relationships of trust with them and with the children. The children accepted her enough to tell her things of importance, to come physically close to her, and to interact respectfully with her. The supervisors trusted her enough to stand back and let her lead when it was her turn to direct the group in activity. Joyce worked continuously throughout the three hours a week that she was there: moving, demonstrating, talking, listening, retrieving, and so forth. In turn, she received something important from the children: within this context, she was genuinely needed by them. As a consequence, she felt like an important person in their lives.

This job-trailing was as successful as any that I observed. Nearly all of them, however, appeared to be qualitatively different from Joyce's. Here is a more typical example of what I observed, particularly among the River City group. Kente is a fourteen-year-old African American whose work placement is at a community center located near his "project" town house.[4]

Kente's supervisor, Ron, greets me and tells Kente to go supervise the younger kids in the gym. There are four or five children there dribbling basketballs. Kente tells one of them to close the door to the outside, which he does. Kente then goes back to the "living room" and watches the basketball game on TV. A girl comes out of the computer room and watches with him. A boy walks by and talks with Kente briefly and then leaves. Kente continues to watch the basketball game on TV. He tells me it's the NBA playoffs. Kente gets up and straightens up the chairs. He enters the adjacent computer room, where he introduces me to his cousin. He then introduces me to his two brothers playing Nintendo at the side of the living room. He goes to the gym to get the vacuum. Kente proceeds to vacuum up a small area and puts the vacuum away.

He sits down and watches the game. Ron calls him into the computer room where he is playing a computer game and tells him to "get busy." Kente tells me that Ron does not want me to see him lazing around. He goes to the gym, gets some cleaning supplies, and cleans up the men's and women's bathrooms.

Kente then returns the cleaning supplies to the gym and shoots some baskets with two friends. Meanwhile, the children whom he was initially asked to supervise are running around playing in an adjacent area. I hear a young child scream. Kente picks him up, comforts him, and then puts his shoe back on. He then rejoins his friends. After a while, Ron comes in and joins in the basketball shooting. He tells Kente to go out and help put away the BBQ, which he does.

Kente then puts some music on and goes to the kitchen to get some donuts to eat. He gets a broom and proceeds to sweep the gym. He goes back to the TV room and talks briefly with his brothers, who are playing Nintendo. He enters the computer room and Ron gives him another work direction. He goes to the gym, where he starts to wash and wax the floor. Then, he interrupts the mopping to go out to the TV room, where he watches a young woman play Nintendo. [He never returns to complete his mopping in the gym—others eventually complete this task for him.] Kente then goes over and watches the basketball game for a while. Ron tells Kente to straighten up the place because he wants to close it soon. Kente gets up from the game and straightens up the chair and picks up some papers. He stops and chats with the young woman at the Nintendo game. He gets the mop and mops the computer room floor. He returns to watch the basketball game on television again. He explains to me that this is not the game that he is interested in.

It is important to understand that Kente's job-trailing at the community center bears no relation to any of the personal career aspirations that he chose for his library research. His stated career interests are drafting and architecture. It was not unusual for placements to be unrelated to career aspirations; such was the case with six of the ten boys in River City. As such, it seems that the link between the interest survey, career research, and job-trailing are tenuous. Two of the boys were given no placement until the last month of the program, and five were placed very late in the year at the local community center as maintenance workers and supervisors. In discussing these observations with Gerald (who was responsible for the placement of all the River City students), he explained that he lacked adequate time to properly complete this job.

The relationship between Kente and Ron can be compared with that between Joyce and her supervisors. Kente and Ron related to each other in an authoritarian-subservient manner, whereas Joyce had a more equal relationship with her supervisors (who, despite the age difference, treated her as a co-worker). On the other hand, Kente was repeatedly being told what to do by Ron. He would never refuse to do a task, but neither would he routinely take the initiative. Jobs would sometimes remain half done while he returned to watching TV or socializing. By contrast, Joyce formed close bonds with the children for whom she was responsible. Kente, although pleasant and caring, would only supervise those younger than himself in a cursory manner. He cared about the children, but not enough to ask them to join him in shooting basketballs. He spoke of the center with pride, but not enough to finish mopping the gym floor. A basketball game on TV took precedence over his work.

These two examples illustrate the various ways OSRP students relate to their work. Precisely why these differences arise is a matter for speculation. Some would argue that Kente and Joyce enter their job-trailings with different attitudes toward work. This is undeniably true. Yet context also makes a difference. Consider some contrasts between these two contexts. Joyce traveled out of her immediate neighborhood to job trail two strangers who were roughly four times her age. After showing her how things are done, they gave her the freedom to develop and implement activities that she personally chose and researched. Kente, on the other hand, walked a few minutes from his house to an environment that was essentially an extension of his family. He worked for a friend of his older brother. His family often used the recreational services. Others in the building were people he has known for years. He routinely used the facility for his own recreation (basketball). As such, Joyce was placed in an environment where she was "stretched" by new experience and Kente was not. To Kente, the center is just an extension of the home. He watches TV at home: why not watch it at the center?

Kente's job-trailing placement is considerably more typical of what I observed than Joyce's. Many were different from Kente's in that the students refused to go to their placements, repeatedly asked for new placements, or were terminated by their supervisors. I often found myself writing that the students are sitting and waiting for somebody to tell them what to do. For numerous reasons, these young people came to experience work as something less than it can be. Many of them failed to become personally involved with the work or with those around them at the work place. Job-trailing became just another OSRP assignment where they earned their minimum wage. This lack of personal involvement was reinforced by Gerald's reaction to students whenever they complained of being bored at their job-trailings. Consider this conversation between myself and Gerald:

BH: You do the best you can to place these kids in the right environment, but is there always going to be a problem in this area?

Gerald: First of all I don't consider it a problem at all, in this area. The job-trailing is the most significant part of what we do with the students, because we're teaching them all these skills and now it's an opportunity to put these skills in the work place. . . . Now whether they're bored to tears or whether they're very active to me is not very relevant. It's them getting there on time, having a dialogue with their supervisor, coming properly dressed: those are the work ethics we're trying to teach here. Because you're going to have a boring job one day. You're going to be sitting behind a desk with nothing to do because no one's calling you on the phone, you're a secretary or something like that. Now how do you handle that? These are the kinds of things we handle in group sessions.

BH: So these kids have got to learn how to handle boredom?

Gerald: Exactly.

Gerald expresses a surprising view of what it means to go to work. I say surprising because it is clear that Gerald is genuinely involved with the work that he himself does. He prides himself on being a self-starter only loosely affiliated with his own boss, who allows him considerable latitude. I never observed Gerald sitting and waiting for somebody else to tell him what to do and doubt that he has ever experienced boredom on the job. So why the double standard? One hint lies in Gerald's reference to the kinds of jobs that these kids are likely to end up with: "you're going to have a boring job one day." He tells students to aspire as high as they can, but apparently expects few to attain rewarding employment. This may help to explain the rather lackluster job-trailings that I observed. The director's role is to assign and supervise most of the job-trailings. His definition of this activity is likely to be communicated to the students and their supervisors. Gerald's attention to form over substance manifests itself in the work sites where young people, for the most part, can be observed following his definition of work.

Classroom Experiences. Classroom practice differs as radically from the formal curriculum as the job-trailing experience does from its idealization. In principle, career training helps each student to develop his or her interests and skills, in order to obtain and keep a satisfying job. In reality, the prevailing attitude toward work is simply incompatible with high career aspirations. The curriculum is trite and irrelevant to career advancement. Students react to it by resisting, that is, with inactivity, attention to form rather than content, and an indulgence in socializing to the exclusion of practically any other activity.

I will first examine the written curriculum as completed in the classroom. The work done by Eric, a fourteen-year-old River City student, will be taken as an example. He is a freshman in the local high school this year, for the second time. He is an average achiever in terms of the OSRP group. Let us look through the three-ringed binder that contains the OSRP classroom work that he produced this year. The most outstanding characteristic of the binder is its brevity. There are almost as many section dividers (14) as there are pages with writing on them (19, not including forms). Of those nineteen pages, five pages contain summaries from the *Dictionary of Occupational Titles*, six are thank-you letters of approximately three sentences each, one is a cover letter to a fictitious employer, and one is a letter to a college requesting information. Louise (the counselor at the River City site) remarks that "even some of the best work really wouldn't be that acceptable in a class that demands grade level work." Conservatively, one would have to describe the written curriculum in practice as "thin" in relation to the number of classroom hours (approximately 275) that OSRP is in session during the year.

Socializing fills many of those classroom hours, but the curriculum in practice also includes other rituals and norms. OSRP rituals include going to the vending machines to get some food and drink; signing in and out of the classroom; going to the cabinet to retrieve and then put away one's work binder; smoking outside the building; making, distributing and eating popcorn (Springfield only); and listening to talks from Mr. Johnson (Gerald) that demand complete student silence. During these talks, Gerald often states behavior expectations, including: dress right for the occasion; give a hearty handshake when you meet someone (of importance) and look them straight in the eye; and talk using standard English (no street talk or swearing). The most often repeated advice from Gerald includes: "aspire as high as you can"; "stay in school and work hard so you can become somebody"; and "first impressions are very important." One of Gerald's most often repeated phrases is, "Don't forget us when you're rich and famous!"

Students find OSRP's written curriculum to be boring and repetitive. They assert that the curriculum in practice is less than it could or should be:

BH: Aren't they giving you the opportunity to experience work?
Obuagu: Nope, not there. Work? That ain't work. That seem like somethin' you do just

because they pay you. You see when somebody do get a job, a real job, they probably act the same way they act at OSRP. Huh.

BH: How do they act at OSRP?

Obuagu: (Laughs) Outrageous. Not normal.

BH: But it's not work?

Obuagu: It ain't work.

BH: If you worked the way people work at OSRP, if you worked that way on the first day of a real job?

Obuagu: You would get fired.

. . .

Yolanda: It's the students. When you got some that's lazy like in OSRP, you got some that come just to get paid and you need some that come to get paid and learn something.

BH: So the staff then are trying?

Yolanda: They trying but you just have some people that won't listen, they don't want to listen.

These two students are representative of others who also express disenchantment with the curriculum in practice. And yet they would never articulate these ideas to the staff—it would be considered rude. They do, however, express these feelings through their actions in the OSRP classroom. Most of the students seem to sense the paradox of participating in a program the main purpose of which is career preparation, but which itself fails to create a work-like atmosphere. In this way, the program rejects the values that it wants to instill in its students. Hard, career-directed work is officially endorsed but unofficially mocked in the day-to-day curriculum. As a result, the students are "bored" and find the atmosphere "unbelievable." They respond by blaming either their "lazy" classmates or the program itself.

As I see it, OSRP does not lack focus or philosophical cohesion. Rather, it lacks the ability to take its own goals seriously and to establish an environment in which the students do the same. Some of the staff see the program in like terms. In addition to observing chaos and a lack of work ethic, these staff recognize other student reactions to the program: a focus on form rather than substance and a resistance to the curriculum itself. Rick is an outsider to the program (on loan from the local Boys and Girls Club). He offers a quasi-staff, quasi-observer perspective. The following comment was made while we were both sitting and observing the group. Without prompting, he turned to me and said:

Rick: Chaos. I think they need more structure. I'm wondering, was it meant to be this way, do you know? I don't see them learning anything. When I talk with the kids, the number one reason they're here is to get paid. They should be learning more, not told what to put down or write in the projects.

Kevin reiterates Rick's observation, from the point of view of a staff member:

Kevin: We govern their behavior in this context, and sometimes they resist with activities like street talk, tone of voice, storming out, not working as assigned, etc. . . . Many of them don't come in with a sincere ethic to work in that class. They come in because it's say, a recreational interlude. And I think their priorities are confused in that sense.

The staff echo the observations of the students. When they see the chaos, however, they tend to focus on the students' resistance and lack of work ethic. They seem unwilling to speculate on the possible relationship between that behavior and a context organized by adults.

It seems clear that classroom experiences for the students are less than ideal. If we consider them in terms of the vocational goals of the program, they are a failure. The observations of staff, students, and this observer coincide: an extremely relaxed work ethic is prevalent in OSRP. The staff and students concur that the curriculum falls below the challenge that is customary even in the students' public school nonacademic-track classes. I have called it thin. Obuagu says it "ain't work." Socializing is the norm, not a concentrated focus on the curriculum. In all likelihood, the two are interrelated: in the absence of a meaningful curriculum, the only thing to do is socialize.

Field Trips. The state curriculum mandates field trips, and OSRP staff willingly comply. In addition, visitors come in to speak on a variety of topics, mostly relating to their careers. Getting out of the classroom is a special event that nearly everybody looks forward to. The trips are planned to expose these "deprived kids" to contexts they would otherwise never experience. Yet there is a significant disjunction between how the staff and the students perceive these special events. Generally, the students are able to circumvent the educational or vocational reasons for the trip or visit. Let us consider one typical example: the overnight trip to State College.

Gerald views these trips as an opportunity for the students to become more familiar with college life. His reasoning is that if college becomes something known and real, this could reinforce his students' educational aspirations. The students, on the other hand, have a different agenda. Here are some of the comments of two college student hosts who agreed to be interviewed at the end of the weekend at State College:

Marlene: Patricia and Joyce [OSRP students] don't really want to be here. They are not interested in the campus life itself, but mainly in partying.

Tim: Louis is interested in partying, but Leon seems much more interested in college, asking questions about different majors, etc.

Marlene: Patricia saw we only take five classes and thought the rest was free. She didn't understand that the rest of the hours are filled up with numerous activities related to the classes. Patricia said they drink, get drunk, party, and relate sexually to guys. I never did this in high school and I'm out of the drinking scene now here. I'm afraid they thought of me as boring.

Tim: Louis came across the same way. He was exposed to drinking, even though he's only in the eighth grade. They came here with a misconception of college as partying.

Marlene: They tell me they go out and party and get drunk every weekend. I didn't do that. I'd go to a friend's house and play a game like Monopoly at that age! Patricia told me that she gets into a bar and goes drinking.

Tim: I wanted to get across that college is a lot of fun and a lot of work, but it is worth it. I don't think I really succeeded in getting this across. I think the program is good, but they have to want to get something out of it besides a pay check. Patricia defines it as a job rather than an experience.

These "middle-class" college hosts cannot help but contrast their adolescent experiences with those of their guests. The lifestyle that includes smoking, drinking, partying, and sex seems alien to them. The hosts' perceptions were that these young people are "out of sync" with the official objectives of the college trip (in addition to student culture).

However, since much of this behavior remains hidden from the staff, they are unlikely to know about it:

Joyce: I've learned to keep my feelings and thoughts away from adults and put on a false front, even though I sometimes wish I could be honest. I've tried being honest: it doesn't work, believe me.

Joyce makes it clear that at least for her, deception of adults is done consciously. She has learned through experience to keep things that adults would not approve of from them. OSRP students saw the college outing as a release from the confines of home and adult supervision. Those of them who looked forward to it anticipated parties, drinking, smoking, and sex. By and large, they were disappointed (as far as I know). What they found was an environment dominated by young people who acted "boring." It became just another part of OSRP.

This kind of scene was repeated time and time again in other field trips. The students would be overtly conformist in the presence of adults, but would try to tailor their participation to their own interests. They adopt the politeness required in public situations, yet often define the adult agenda as irrelevant. Here, as in the written curriculum and the job-trailing, form wins out over substance. Adult conceptions are successfully kept at a distance.

Goal #3: Counseling

The formal curriculum calls for regularly scheduled group and individual counseling sessions (the latter to take between one half hour and two hours per student per week). Practice never remotely resembled that statement of intent. In fact, the discrepancy between a perceived reasonable minimum amount of counseling and the amount regularly occurring in the program compelled Louise (the River City counselor) to hand in her resignation at the end of the year. Gerald believed that the River City group was falling behind in the written curriculum. He decided that all counseling was to cease as of January, with the counselor becoming a second educator. This was to be a temporary measure until the group caught up. As it happened, this never occurred. Predictably, this did not sit well with Louise. As background to her comments, I should mention that Gerald was the sole staff member with the River City students during the months of July and August. When the rest of the staff came back in September, he returned to his administrative role as director:

BH: Were you experiencing some success with them, do you think?
Louise: Yes. I was having individual sessions with them and group sessions. . . . And it takes about five or six sessions before they start expressing themselves and feeling a

little bit safe and knowing the routine and they were to the point where they were going to start dealing with some things that matter to them. And that's when it was all stopped [by Gerald]. . . . I still think it's because he had that close relationship in the summer. And that he couldn't separate himself, he couldn't abide. Because he had trouble enough with it the year before, but we successfully kept him out of our hair. Because he never really had his foot all the way in with the kids. That made it hard. Makes it very difficult.

Louise is arguing that Gerald feels a certain ownership of the kids' loyalty that he develops during the summer. She believes that he terminated her counseling because it competed with his special relationship with these young people. The salient point is that the curriculum in practice in this area (as in the others) departs significantly from the formal curriculum. Counseling, like job-trailing and OSRP classroom experiences, is an element of programming that fails to live up to images outlined in the formal curriculum.

CONCLUSION

OSRP, then, is a program that the state endorses as a success, and yet fails to accomplish its central goals. This chapter has identified some of the factors that may be responsible for this program's failure, including lack of staff time (possibly related to inadequate funding), ambiguous job-trailing organization, weak written curriculum, and special events that do not truly engage students. In chapter 1, I outlined a perspective of compensatory education that argues that many of these programs have the potential to succeed if enough planning and resources are poured into them. Some readers might agree with that perspective, arguing that Gerald and his staff have made tactical mistakes, that if corrected, would likely turn OSRP into a success. Some might blame the personal outlook of individual staff members for program weaknesses. Further, some might argue that increased funding would make a positive contribution to OSRP outcomes.

However, in subsequent chapters, it will become evident that OSRP's inability to realize its goals is more related to ideological and staff-student relational issues than to the above-mentioned elements. I found an underlying set of attitudes among staff members about the nature of the program that make its inability to fulfill its goals inevitable. I call that set of beliefs a "conservative ideology of hope." Future chapters will explain the precise meaning of this set of ideas, and will show how it impacts upon OSRP curriculum in practice. Once some of the hidden underlying perspectives and practices within OSRP are better understood, it will be clear that superficial changes in programming or personnel are unlikely to produce positive outcomes.

NOTES

1. Core subjects include English, mathematics, science, and social science. The reported changes in grades were obtained by subtracting students' final numeric grades in the four core subjects from their grades as reported on their first term grade report. Note that the total column does not add up to 100 percent because of rounding.

2. There was one regular exception: Raquel would frequently come in and do homework, alone among the Springfield group.

3. The students are supervised at the sites by employers or employees who agree to allow one or more of these young people to work under them. The organization benefits from the services of this young person at no cost.

4. I made these observations of Kente on 5/9/92. This is an edited version of my field notes.

3

A Conservative Ideology of Hope

In the previous chapter I concluded that OSRP is not able to achieve its goal of motivating its students to integrate within the school system. This in itself is not surprising, given the research on schools and how they relate to many lower-class and minority students (chapter 1). In this chapter, I will begin to answer the question: Why does OSRP fail? The answer concentrates on the importance of culture and context in shaping people's thinking, and in subsequently helping to mold behavior patterns. From my first observations, I was struck by the importance of a set of ideas as the driving force behind this program. I call these beliefs "the conservative ideology of hope." They are imparted most visibly in Gerald's frequent addresses to the students. This transmission of ideas is noticeably effective because he is such a dominant and charismatic figure within the program. He is youthful, energetic, and articulate in expressing this ideology. He symbolically encapsulates his thinking in a large banner that sits at the front of both OSRP classrooms: Success = Opportunity & Effort. The perspective also permeates curriculum in practice because Gerald initiates most of the program planning. This chapter explores the precise nature and quality of this ideology. In subsequent chapters, it will be pointed out that this set of beliefs has important repercussions for the staff and students alike. These convictions influence the degree to which the program can expect to be successful in meeting its goals.

The chapter is divided into two main sections. The first will present the program's conservative ideology of hope, as understood by the staff, students, and parents. In this exploration, it will be shown that although there is general adherence to a mainstream ideological perspective, there are minority positions that coexist alongside the dominant one. However, Gerald's key role in organizing and influencing programming diminishes the visibility of these alternative beliefs. The second section explores some of the structures both within and outside the program that help to tie OSRP staff and students to the dominant ideology. We will see why alternative viewpoints are not prevalent within OSRP.

OSRP'S CONSERVATIVE IDEOLOGY OF HOPE

It is important to understand the meaning of the three terms that I have used to describe OSRP's core ideas: "conservative," "ideology," and "hope." OSRP's ideology may be thought of as conservative in the sense that it imagines a coincidence of interests between the individual (even the disadvantaged individual) and his or her society. It is also conservative because social institutions are given priority over individualism. Values espoused by the church and the traditional patriarchal family are given preference within OSRP, that is, belief in hierarchy, loyalty, and authority. Conservatives believe in traditional institutions and values because of their concern that chaos may emerge if individuals question the natural/institutional order of things (Nisbet, 1952). Because institutions are viewed in this manner, they are presented within the program as being beyond public reproach.

When I use the term ideology here, I am referring to ideas or beliefs that help people understand how our society's system of social stratification functions. It is a set of mental representations about class that people implicitly or explicitly hold. We may imagine these ideas as being borrowed or interpreted from culture and acquired from personal discussion, books, the media, the schools, as well as youth programs and other social institutions. One of the questions that is implicitly raised by this concept is the degree to which the ideas of the ruling class make their way to the bottom of the stratification system. Does control over legitimate social institutions permit the ruling class to successfully inculcate their idealizations of material relationships to disadvantaged, at-risk youth? The data in this chapter will help us understand how OSRP members perceive society's system of distribution of economic rewards, that is, its opportunity structures and routes of gaining socioeconomic mobility.

OSRP's ideology is hopeful in that it assumes that opportunity exists for anyone in society. This is because social institutions are thought of as orderly and rational, using meritocratic criteria in the distribution of scarce rewards. It is posited that if the individual follows a specific approach, he or she will be appropriately rewarded with upward social and economic mobility. This is the basic message that Mr. McDermott (a representative from the state funding agency) delivered to OSRP at the year-end awards ceremony, and that program staff articulated in their interviews:

Mr. McD: We are still the richest country in the world, filled with opportunity. Some of us feel we are unable to take advantage of the opportunities available. . . . The secret is to set goals and work toward them, take the tunnel vision approach. Here is an analogy. Let us imagine two ships in a harbor. On one of them, the captain and crew plan their destination, carefully charting direction, time and speed. The chances are 99 per cent that they will reach that destination. Now imagine another ship where the captain allows the winds to guide the ship wherever they desire. The chances are almost nil that they will end up where they desire. If you follow my advice and act like the first captain, good luck will be attracted to you. Don't be influenced by negative influences. . . . All things are possible to those who believeth. (Field note)

. . .

Kevin: Unquestioned. This is the best country in the world. I've been to a lot of societies. I have seen inside. I have been places these kids probably will never go in their lifetime. This is, without question, the best opportunity they'll ever have. The best country in the world. . . . This country has tremendous plethora of opportunity. What about children coming over here, can't speak English, and within months, within years, they not only grab our system, but they achieve. They're on their way to unparalleled success in this country, okay?

Since our society is seen as being full of opportunity, this ideology must include an explanation for failure. Generally, the staff blame the failures on OSRP students and their parents. For example, Gerald explains failure in terms of students' poor skill development:

Gerald: I've discovered that they're leaving school more than ever. Their basic skill development is poor. They can't present themselves well. They can't write. Their presentation skills again are terrible and then we're asking them to be ready for the work force and they're not ready.

. . .

Jane: Parents and students, and I use this word loosely, are stupid because it's there for the taking and they're so dumb. . . . They're too dumb to make their kids go to school. . . . They're just too dumb to take advantage of what is there for them. And they're too dumb to work hard for it.

The majority of the staff, then, view society as being open to all its members. Since some neglect to take advantage of this open system, their failure must be due to personal defects or imperfections. When one considers the failure that the staff members encounter in relation to their students (chapter 2), it is easy to understand why they might be dependent upon "hope." They hope that somehow their efforts will turn things around for a youngster or two. What else could they do with people who are dumb, have poor skill development, are negative, and lack motivation?

It is significant that two staff members hold an alternative conception of our social stratification system. However, neither of these persons present their alternative position in a manner that has any visible impact upon the program. Stanley, as the site administrator, adopts a hands-off approach, allowing Gerald to run his own program. Louise was overwhelmed by Gerald's energy and his agenda. This eventually culminated in her resigning from the program at the end of the year:

Stanley: And I hate to bring up things like, you know, sports or things of that nature. But once equity and parity and opportunity were open fully to the minority community, they excelled in that line of work. And I think we need to do that across all spectrums. . . . We develop a very, very comprehensive athletic preparation system within this country to move minorities through this system. But we don't do the same for minorities within the career fields, within what I would say are the educational fields. . . . Because there's a big business in today's sports environment. You know, it's a revenue-oriented decision.

. . .

Louise: Generally I feel as though the state is satisfied with the status quo. I think River
  City in particular is very satisfied with the status quo.

BH: I'm sorry, but I don't understand what you mean by that.

Louise: Of who achieves and who doesn't. In our school system, who gets the jobs and
  who doesn't here in our city. It would only add to the competition if more students started
  to achieve and compete for the jobs. So maybe in turn it's not that hard to believe that the
  state also wouldn't be that unhappy.

BH: Is it a racial issue or is it a class issue or is it both?

Louise: I think it's both.

BH: So then why would the state foot the dollars that go into this program?

Louise: Prevent problems like racial tension and so on.

Stanley and Louise are alone among the staff in perceiving that our society may be
composed of antagonistic groups based on class or race. They perceive that these
groups have differing access to power within society, and that this may be an
important factor in understanding why so many OSRP students do not achieve within
the school context. They do not blame the victims or their parents for failing to take
advantage of opportunities made available to them. Instead, they blame social
institutions for failing to offer them the same opportunities open to other groups.
Because these two staff members rarely communicate with each other, they have
never recognized their similar perspectives on this issue. As such, their alternative
viewpoint has never gained any momentum within the organization.

The students generally follow the lead of the staff with respect to ideological
orientation. This is particularly true at the River City location, where Gerald's nearby
physical presence and his energetic personality have an overwhelming influence on
a daily basis. Listen to these "disadvantaged" African American youngsters as they
explain their perceptions of our stratification system. They speak almost as if they
have one voice:

Argina: I think that if they work hard enough in school and in college that they be able to
  get a good job. But if they don't, then if they don't work good in college and school they
  won't get a good job. They get a job working at A & P or something.

                                        • • •

BH: Why do you go to school every day?

LaKesia: To get a education so I can get out of high school, graduate, and go to college.

BH: Why is that important?

LaKesia: Cause I don't want to be some bum on the street. I wanna get a education. I
  want ta be a educated person.

                                        • • •

BH: You've told me that you don't like going to school. So why do you keep going?

Obuagu: So I can be somebody in life. . . . With the way things are today, if you don't go to
  school, either you gonna end up on the streets or dead.

BH: So this is a serious matter.

Obuagu: Ya.

BH: You are forced to go to a place that you don't like or else end up in a place you don't like.

Obuagu: Ya.

. . .

Kente: Most people can hardly read the newspaper. The people that's getting shot or shot somebody, they dropped out of high school, they sellin' dope, stuff like that. You can tell right there. Bad example that you drop out of school. You ain't got the jobs, could be dead-end jobs, ain't gonna get you nowhere. Only way you want to get somewhere is by gettin' an education.

. . .

Yolanda: Ya. That's all you got to do now is to learn cause if you don't learn nothin' then you're not goin' to get no diploma or nothin and you ain't goin to find no good job. . . . Cause without it you end up on the streets.

These young people have a sense of urgency in their voices. Living on the street is not a frivolous concern. Their fears also include being a bum or "getting shot or [shooting] somebody." They see one sure ticket out: education. It guarantees them distance between themselves and these apprehensions. In addition, school helps them "get somewhere," "have good things," and "be somebody in life." They agree with the staff message encouraging them to see their present behaviors in school as being intimately linked to their future occupational success.

I asked these young people about the possibility that various barriers would interfere with their career goals. I was interested in finding out just how open they really thought the society was to them. Could their race or gender interfere with their paths to success? What about their school placement within nonacademic tracks? I heard the same answers over and over again.

Racial and Gender Barriers

BH: Do you think that they [people who are sexist or racist] could hold you back from success in the future?

Felicia: Ain't gonna hold me back cause I'm gonna fight all the way as far as I can. So if they have a problem with it, I hope they ain't doin' it when I get up there. . . . But if they do, I'll have a little talk with them!

. . .

BH: Do you think that this [racism or sexism] will be a problem for you?

LaKesia: No, cause everybody gets along with me.

. . .

Argina: But if they do that, the black person can take the company to court. Cause it's a law about doin' that.

School Tracking Barriers

Maria: I'm in general [track] in everything.

BH: Do you think that that's helpful to you or in some way hurtful to you?

Maria: I think it's uh, it's just my mentality. I see no problem with it. Uh, and it helps me because it gives me time to learn and to think.

BH: Do you think it might help you or hurt you in terms of getting a career?

Maria: I think, uh, I don't think that it would hurt me at all.

BH: Do you think that you could attend a college with general subjects?

Maria: I would say so. I mean, why not?

(Maria is a nonacademic track student who aspires to be a counselor)

. . .

BH: Do you think that taking general level courses will help you or hinder you in your future?

LaKesia: Help me in my future. Cause by me takin' like general if I take general and it get easier then I can move up a level and it just help me more in college.

(LaKesia is a nonacademic track student who aspires to be a nurse)

. . .

BH: Do you have a sense that taking basic [track] classes might not allow you to get into a college to get that training [to become a recreational therapist]?

Argina: No. No, I don't feel that way. They would, the college should anyway. Because, you know, I goin' to get my high school records and all that.

(Argina is a special education student who aspires to be a recreational therapist)

These discussions of racial, gender, and school track barriers to occupational success reflect OSRP students' belief that society is open to upward mobility of all young people. From the perspective of the educational research on barriers (chapter 1), these River City students are nothing short of wildly optimistic. Their answers reveal a naiveté about how colleges select from candidates and about what kind of skills have currency in our educational marketplace. This is a version of the staff's ideology of hope—a faith that somehow everything will work out. The majority of Springfield students share this perspective. It is significant, however, that an alternative ideology is shared by four students at this site. It varies from Terry and Jen's mild questioning of the value of school grades to Patricia and Nick's near-total rejection of the fairness of the meritocratic and credentialing nature of our stratification system:

Terry: I think marks are very important. But I think in the long run when you are in the work force, I think what you've learned is going to help you more than just letter grades in school.

. . .

Jen: I think that if you have a lot of common sense, numbers don't matter. Numbers and letters on paper don't matter. It's what you have up in your head, and how you use it.

. . .

Patricia: At seventeen I can drop out of school, and I can make as much money as my uncle is making when I turn eighteen.

Nick: How much is he making?

Patricia: He's making fifteen dollars an hour.

Nick: Doin' what?

Patricia: He's painting plumbing things.

Nick: So what are you gonna do?

Patricia: I'm goin' into real estate. There's good money in that, too. Cause some of the jobs out here you don't need a diploma.

. . .

Leon: The more education they get, the more, the easier their job's goin' to make it.

Patricia: That ain't true. Cause people now who are graduating are having a hard time. They had it right on TV. They're havin' a hard time finding a job.

Leon: It's not going to be like that in the future though.

Nick: There's goin' to be no jobs in the future. It's all goin' to be computerized. This world sucks.

. . .

BH: You said to me to prepare for a job, you could just go to a job site and learn the skills at that site.

Nick: Ya, but then you have to have all this background which I think is bull.

BH: So you don't really think you could get yourself employed in a job that you would really like without graduating from high school?

Nick: Well, you have to graduate to have this job, but what if you're good at it and one of the best around, but didn't graduate? That makes no sense to me at all. . . . I don't agree with any of that stuff. I don't understand. . . . A teacher would treat some students and some other students like favorites. He would favor this kid and that would get me mad, cuz he has no reason. Like God put us on this earth to be treated equal. But then there's people bein' treated better than others for no reason at all cuz that's the way they are. Like cuz one could be rich, one could be poor. Who do you think is gonna get treated better? The rich person. Cuz the other person is poor and doesn't have nice clothes. Like people that are, what is that, prejudice.

Nick, Patricia, and to a lesser extent, Jen, and Terry are the only OSRP students offering a critique (or are at least a questioning) of the prevailing conservative ideology of hope. Nick and Patricia are arguing that the schools do not fairly assign students to the job market based on grades. According to them, other nonmeritocratic criteria are presently considered within schools, as well as in job attainment and success within one's career. Patricia, Jen, and Terry argue that nonschool criteria are also important in career success. Patricia asserts that our occupational structure is undergoing such profound change that her future is uncertain. Nick questions the very existence of a meritocracy by suggesting that class and race are factors in staff treatment of students within schools. Yet this kind of critique of the program's prevailing ideology is rare among the students (notice Leon attempting to defend the ideology of hope). It is significant that this type of critique is completely undetectable among the River City students, where one might expect the additional fact of racial oppression to play out in this way. I will come back to this question in the next section, where the factors that bind OSRP staff and students to the dominant ideology are discussed.

STRUCTURES BINDING OSRP MEMBERS TO THE DOMINANT IDEOLOGY

This segment will consider the forces attracting OSRP staff and students to the program generally and to its ideology more specifically. The participants in the program can be seen as reacting reasonably to a series of structures that encourage them to see things in specific ways. These factors should not be seen as deterministic. Rather, they are conditions in the environment that invite certain subjective responses on the part of OSRP members. The first part of this section discusses forces influencing the staff's adherence to the ideology of hope. The last part focuses on the students' loyalty to this same ideology.

The Staff

There are a number of factors affecting the staff in their relationship to the prevailing ideology of hope: they are influenced by their religious/quasi-religious orientations, their relations with Gerald, and by U.S. culture. Together, these factors help to encourage the staff to conform to the program's ideology of hope.

The staff as a group consider their religious beliefs to be influential in shaping their lives generally, including their participation in the program. The one staff member who is not religious has a public service commitment to the program that closely mirrors the religious outlook of his colleagues. These religious and public service ideals support the conservative ideology of hope:

Gerald: Let's put it this way, there are some people who feel that there are Christian beliefs in serving your fellow man. I guess in that way, if you look at the Christian belief, then I would share that feeling. . . . I believe that I should be in a place where I could feel that I'm making a difference in someone's life. That's an avid Christian belief. That you're serving, that you have a true sense of service, that you're helping someone, you're changing their life, you're making an impact, you're serving as a role model.

. . .

Tim: The Lord always said that each of us has our own talents. . . . I have a talent to work with young people. I had even before I got involved in the counseling field. And I find a sincere interest in helping them better themselves, whatever that might be. So from that, I'm taking the talent that God gave me. And when He asks me to report back, hopefully I'll have something that I can [say, i.e., that] I've expanded my talents to help those others.

. . .

Kevin: Now religion is at the center point of my life. I attend church every Sunday. It gives me purpose, purpose of my soul. It helps define my role to contribute to animate and inanimate objects around me. We have to respect and preserve things as well as possible. They all deserve to be treated with dignity and sensitivity. Religion makes me want to contribute to humanity. I'd like to leave a legacy of positive values.

This is a staff for whom religion is an important factor in helping to shape their relationship with the program and the young people within it. They share a public service ideal, that is, a sense that one has an obligation to help those less privileged than oneself. These staff members want to make a difference, explain life for them, or leave a legacy to help OSRP students better themselves. They accept an individualistic model that assumes that OSRP can save a small number of deprived students, and that this is a worthwhile act in and of itself. There is little or no recognition that social structures may impact negatively upon these students and others like them. The staff view themselves as the loving agents of God (or society) who assist in a positive resocialization process.

In addition, the staff are working in an environment that allows them little freedom to deviate from Gerald's programmatic structures. This is especially true of the River City staff who work in close proximity to Gerald's office. Listen to the staff talk about what it is like to work for Gerald:

Kevin: He established structure, which I thought was essential, and that's good. But the structure didn't have a built-in flex margin. It was everything by the letter, to the "T." And that's fine, but there isn't much opportunity for me to step forward and say, "Okay now, this is what I'd like to add conjunctively with the prescriptions in this program." And he didn't allow me much creative license to do anything. Everything was predetermined by himself. . . . He was chief cook, bottle washer, maitre d'.

BH: Well, what role did that leave you?

Kevin: (long silence) Well, that's my answer. That pause, that pregnant pause is my answer.

• • •

Louise: But he [Gerald] couldn't just let Kevin develop a relationship with the students either. He had to constantly interrupt, constantly interrupt, constantly interrupt. . . . Kevin and I used to make plans together. What we would do and how we would do it. But they started to be interrupted. We'd walk in and we'd be told that something else completely different had to be done. So ya, it's gotten to be where Gerald simply runs the complete show.

• • •

Jane: Oh Gerald, he's nice, he's my kid too. I can't disappoint him. He's my big, he's just like a big

BH: Kid?

Jane: Kid. And he has, he places so much importance in these things, and [he's always saying], "Exciting, isn't this exciting!"

BH: Oh, I know it.

Jane: And he's always tapping. Okay, okay Gerald, it's wonderful. And I revel in your happiness over it. And he's my boss. I'm not gonna argue with him. No.

BH: You don't say, "This is a dumb idea?"

Jane: No, because I don't want to make him feel bad.

In a word, the staff perceive Gerald as controlling, allowing others little or no space in which to interpret curriculum. They are there to carry out his initiatives. As a result, Kevin and Louise have come to define their jobs as "a part-time commitment" rather than something freely chosen as a medium of self-expression. Jane also feels dominated by Gerald, but to a lesser extent. Because of the several miles between her site and Gerald's, his invasiveness is limited to isolated incidents. Jane accepts Gerald's leadership with the justification that she should be practicing what she preaches to the students, that is, to accept a boss's right to define the work setting.

Gerald's "excitement" factor also limits the development of alternative perspectives or ideologies within the program. Jane mentions that she cannot deflate his always inflated balloon. She calls him "a big kid" who is always so excited. I suspect that Gerald's presentation of self plays a part in protecting him from being questioned or challenged by staff. Appearing to be overly enthusiastic reduces the chance that others will contest his decisions (and thereby deflate his enthusiasm). As such, Gerald's self-presentation may add to ideological uniformity within the group.

It is clear that OSRP is very much Gerald's program. It is not a collaborative effort among professionals, with each having his or her own contribution to make to programming. Because of this top-down organization, the staff are bound to represent Gerald's ideological understandings, simply because he is the program. He controls. He supervises. He plans. There is little room for any one else to compete effectively. If staff disagree with him, they do what Kevin and Louise and others have done before them at the River City site: they resign or fail to return the following year. In short, the staff are closely tied to Gerald's conservative ideology of hope simply because the day-to-day working environment permits little deviation.

From Gerald's perspective, he has good reason to believe in this ideology and to be dominant in his relations with his staff. He openly and repeatedly presents himself as proof that everybody can make it in America. His personal biography as the lower-class African American son of an alcoholic, abusive father and a mother who worked at menial labor is paramount in his thinking about America's opportunity structure. He reasons that if he could take advantage of opportunities that were available to become a success, others can also do the same. As a result, I often heard him giving young people advice that flows logically from this kind of experience and perspective: take advantage of opportunity programs, stay in school, try hard, and you will become somebody. He believes fervently in this message, taking every available opportunity to proselytize it. This fervency and the energy that allowed him to rise out of the ghetto also manifest themselves in a tendency to control staff and students within the program. He commits his entire self to this work and does not permit individuals to stand in his way. Hence, Gerald's control of OSRP and his endorsement of its official ideology reflect his experiences and beliefs, leaving other staff members little room to create alternative visions as a basis for programming.

Last, the overriding explanation for the prevalence of the ideology of hope among the program staff is that dominant U.S. culture provides them with an influential set of ideas that closely approximates this perspective. It has often been observed that American culture promulgates a belief in individual achievement. For example, Ryan (1971) argues that Americans overwhelmingly believe in the appealing notion of their country as a land of opportunity. He calls this a belief in "fair play," where individuals who display ability and directed effort are thought to deserve greater resources from an essentially fair system of distributing social rewards. From this perspective, OSRP staff appear to have simply internalized their country's dominant ideological position.

The Students

With the exception of the few Springfield students mentioned above, OSRP students believe in the program's ideology of hope. This is surprising in that it tends to contradict findings from other ethnographic studies of lower-class or African American students who are often found to adopt ideologies of resistance (McLeod, 1987; Ogbu, 1974, 1978; Willis, 1977). Why do OSRP students adopt the program's conservative ideology of hope? In answering this question, three factors will be examined. First, the students benefit from the program and generally support it. Second, they lack any alternative ideological influences at home. And last, the River City students genuinely look up to and idealize Gerald. This is also true of the Springfield group, but to a lesser extent. This identification makes the students listen to him, seek to please him, and accept his ideology.

The program achieves an 80 percent attendance rate for a variety of reasons. Most important, OSRP pays its students the legal minimum hourly wage for the time that they attend. In addition, the program imposes minimal academic and behavioral demands, represents a time for socializing with peers, and for some, provides relief from the boredom of returning home after school every day. Consider some of the responses of the students to my question, "Why do you attend OSRP?"

Joyce: Well, I need the money.
BH: That's an honest answer.
Joyce: I like my friends here. Some of them are okay, my little group.

. . .

Raquel: Cause of the money.
BH: Do you think the money's pretty important?
Raquel: Uh huh. I mean I could buy stuff I want now instead of askin' my mom when she doesn't really have it.

. . .

Latoya: But since I been in this program I been earning my own money and this year I buy all my clothes and my school supplies and I even help my mother out a little bit when she needs a little bit of money or whatever. I've helped her out, so I've changed in that sense.

. . .

Felicia: The pay, it's important, but it's not really that important. But that's not the only reason I come. I come because I want to make something of myself. I come for the money too, but, but I want all of it. Other than that, if it wasn't a check coming in, I'd still come to the program because I just want to make something of myself. If, and if I do make something of myself then in the future I will be getting a check anyways.

There are a variety of factors occurring to bind the students to the program. Most say that the pay is not enough to keep them coming over the long haul (even though there are those who guess that the program attendance would be devastated by eliminating payment). Those who enjoy the pay indicate some of the uses to which it is put. Aside from the pay, students also come because they identify the program with upward mobility, with learning, and with social contact with peers. These are all things that they value. And their positive valuation of these characteristics tends to manifest itself in a reasonably positive attitude toward the program as a whole.

Another reason why the students seem to accept the program ideology is because they have heard these ideas in their culture. I have no direct evidence of their schools' or the media's roles in this area, but I did question their parents about their views of the stratification system. I asked each parent about his or her hopes for his or her child's future. What emerged was spoken concern for upward mobility.

Springfield Parents

BH: What do you think Jen will be doing when she leaves high school?
Jen's mom: Ah, well hopefully, she can get further education like she said she wanted to work with children. I know, you know hopefully she can find something that she can build on and that.
BH: Where would she get training for that kind of child care work? What kind of a place would you imagine her going to?
JM: I don't know. I'd like to see her go to [local] community college if I could. Ya.
BH: Umhm. Do you think that that's likely?
JM: I'm not, I'm not sure.

. . .

BH: Do you think that he'll graduate from high school?
Nick's mom: I can pray that he does. I hope he does. I think he's back on the right track now. I'm hoping.

. . .

BH: What do you think is likely to happen to her? Do you think that she's going to graduate from high school?
Nancy's mom: Well as long as I'm alive she will. That's one of the things that I'm real, I'm real, you know, I worry about all that because, just (pause)
BH: Well it's normal for parents to worry about that. But do you think that you're more worried than the average parent?
NM: Ya, because I think Nancy is a lot like I am. And when I was fifteen, I was pregnant.

River City Parents

BH: What do you think Wateef will do when he leaves school?
Wateef's dad: Are you talking about high school?
BH: High school, ya. Do you think he'll go on in his studies?

WD: There's no doubt in my mind about it. He's gonna definitely do it. Definitely.

• • •

BH: What do you think that Obuagu will be doing when he leaves high school?
Obuagu's aunt: Uh, we've talked about him going into the service, furthering his education, going to college. That's a definite. He's definite about that. Education is very important to him.

• • •

BH: Do you think that she will graduate from high school and go on to college?
Shalimar's mom: Ya.
BH: What would you like to see her do?
SM: I'd like her to graduate from high school and go to college.
BH: Any idea about what kind of a career you would prefer for her?
SM: Well, she's got her heart set on being a dermatologist. So, it's gonna be right along with her. I hope she makes it.
BH: Do you think she can make that goal?
SM: I think she can do it. If she put her mind to it, she can do it.

Like the program staff, the parents want upward mobility for their children. However, the Springfield and River City parents differ in their thinking about the likelihood that their children will complete their schooling and go on to successful careers. The Springfield parents use the word "hope" repeatedly in discussing their children's future, emphasizing the hopeful part of OSRP's ideology. River City's African American parents feel much more positive about their children's prospects for graduating from high school, attending college, and obtaining the career of their choice. This attitude seems optimistic, considering their children's school grades, track position, and the existence of racial and gender barriers (see chapters 1 and 2). River City parents believe that their children can make the educational and occupational systems work for them. And it seems that OSRP plays a role in their optimism. They perceive that the program has inspired their children to want to achieve and become somebody:

Quionna's mom: I think it's a good program, you know. They help them. . . . It's helping her to find out who she is and what she wants to do. She's planning on going to college. She's been really interested in going to college. She talks about it all the time.

• • •

BH: So you think the program has helped her focus more on school and a possible career?
Yolanda's mom: I, I think so. Not only that. Because of the kinds of field trips that they have been on with OSRP. For example, going up to the different, to the colleges. And being there on campus. As far as the black children are concerned, I see them doing for them. I'm only speaking in that respect. It gives them something to be able to shoot for. They have like a black role model to them to say that I can do it.

These African American parents understand OSRP to be a program that offers a special opportunity to their children, making them optimistic about future upward mobility. They openly endorse the program's ideology, focusing on individual upward mobility.

Thus, there is a coincidence of interests between the parents and the official ideology of the program. The parents want the same things for their children that the program promises: individual upward mobility through education and career planning. The students see a chorus of adults around them saying the same things: "Think ahead to a career, plan for your future, concentrate on your school work, make me proud of you." (paraphrase)

The last structure helping to bind the students to the program's ideology is the quality of the relationship that they have with the two most prominent staff members, Gerald and Mrs. H. There are qualitative differences between the two groups in this regard, so they will be considered separately. The River City students simply adore Gerald (whom they refer to as Mr. Johnson). The boys appear to look up to him as a role model and the girls seem to love him as a father figure. There is something magical in these relationships:

Shalimar: He's like marvelous. He's great. I think he's a great man.

                                              • • •

Dewitt: Mr. Johnson? He's nice . . . caring . . . cool.

                                              • • •

Kente: Uh, he a nice man. Nice, nice. He really care about the students here and you can really tell too. He ain't selfish.

                                              • • •

Chalka: Mr. Johnson is real cool because he doesn't ignore me. I talk to him about my problems.

                                              • • •

Latoya: I could be totally honest with Mr. Johnson. I feel I could tell Mr. Johnson anything.

These youngsters respect Gerald. They see personal qualities in him that combine an aura of self-confidence, an honest display of caring about individuals, flexibility in dealing with individuals, being "cool," and giving them his time. In return, they give him their sincere affection and loyalty. It is a significant accomplishment that not one student in the River City program expresses an alternative perspective. Because Gerald means so much to them, they respond favorably when he repeatedly espouses his ideology of individual mobility.

The Springfield group have a different position when it comes to personal loyalty to staff. Let us consider their feelings about Gerald and Mrs. H., in turn:

Gerald.
Joyce: Mr. Johnson? He's cool. Ya, I like him.

. . .

Patricia: Ya, he's a cool person. He, uh, he was boring on that trip [to the college] though. I don't know. Something must have hit him.

. . .

BH: What about Mr. Johnson?
Terry: Uhm, I don't know. Mr. Johnson's kind of, he's a nice guy but he kind of gets to me sometimes.
BH: In what way?
Terry: Uhm. He, I think he, he uh has a lot of favoritism.
BH: Toward the River City group?
Terry: Ya. Definitely. A lot of my friends who are in the group with me don't like to put up with it. I have to hear their side and I agree with it.

. . .

Josh: I think Mr. Johnson should stop being so racial.
BH: You think he's prejudiced against whites?
Josh: Yep. He is.

Mrs. H. (Jane).
Jen: Well, she's a substitute in school. She really gets on my case in school. That's really embarrassing when she like yells at me in school. Which she has no right really to do, because it has nothing to do with school. It has to do with work [OSRP]. And that really embarrasses me. But like, when I go to work I don't really want to talk to her because she's embarrassed me, and I don't want to say anything to her.

. . .

Joyce: She's too, I don't know, motherlike. She drives people nuts. And she gets on your case. And like if she's subbing in school and you do something at work [OSRP], then she brings it all in there. And I don't think that's fair.

. . .

Terry: She's patient and tolerant.
BH: More than she should be, or . . .
Terry: Uhm, sometimes. But I appreciate it, I appreciate it.
BH: So how do you see her being very patient and tolerant?
Terry: I think she puts up with a lot more than she should.

. . .

Patricia: To be honest with you, I cannot stand Mrs. H. And she may be nice, but she is a witch. She is a total witch.
BH: What makes you think that?
Patricia: Because she, she, I don't know. I hate it when she yells. Oh God. Please have mercy on me, you know? It's like, just shut up.

The Springfield students only give Gerald mixed reviews. There is a feeling among many of them that he favors the River City kids over themselves in the extra attention and perks that he is able to bestow upon them. At one point, they developed a grievance list to present to him, containing complaints such as:

- he pays the River City kids for field trips while we do not get paid for them;
- we always have to go there for meetings, they never come to our site;
- they have optional paid Saturday classes and we don't; and
- some of their kids still attend after-school sports, while this is forbidden to us.

These and other grievances remain alive in the Springfield students' minds. They reduce Gerald's credibility in their eyes to the point where some of them openly accuse him of being racial and showing favoritism.

Mrs. H. also suffers from mixed comments. She cares about these young people and communicates that caring openly and honestly. But therein also lies the downfall in her relationship with them. Because she sees herself as their surrogate mother, she takes liberties in yelling at them and embarrassing them in public situations. This means that in addition to receiving favorable evaluations from her students, she also receives comments that show students' objections to her yelling and over-mothering. As Joyce commented to me, "I already have one mother, what would I want another one for?"

From these mixed reviews of their two major staff persons, we can see that the Springfield students experience OSRP differently from the River City group. Clearly, the latter are more inclined to experience the program as a personal identification with a strong and respected leader of their own race. For the Springfield group, both leaders get a mixed reception at best. This is associated with significantly different identification of self with the program as a whole. To the River City students, OSRP is a major part of their lives. In Springfield, however, there is compartmentalization of the program as a more or less boring "job" with a domineering boss whose presence must be endured in order to get paid. The result is a noticeable difference in the students' personal belief in the program's conservative ideology of hope. The River City group takes it as literal gospel because it is uttered from a revered person's lips and is personified in his program. On the other hand, the Springfield students feel more freedom to reinterpret the program ideology in light of their own experiences. This is what allows students like Terry, Jen, Patricia, and Nick to speak out comfortably against the program ideology in Springfield (while I could find nobody who would do so in River City).

CONCLUSION

This chapter has described two things. First, it clarified the program's conservative ideology of hope. Briefly, this means that OSRP actively supports a view of our society as being open to all, irrespective of race, social class, gender, and so forth. This view implicitly holds that society is organized by a set of rules that, if followed, promises to benefit all. It also implicitly accepts the benign nature of this set of rules or social contract.

Second, it was argued that structural conditions exist within the program and outside the program to bind the staff and the students to this mainstream ideology. The staff's ideology is shaped by their religious and/or public service ideals, by the fact that the director is energetic and controlling, and by dominant U.S. culture. Most students see themselves as benefiting from the program because of its steady pay, minimal academic and behavioral demands, and their strong relationship with the director. In addition, their parents believe in the same basic ideology, no doubt communicating this set of understandings to their children. These factors are seen as predisposing most students to believe in the conservative ideology of hope.

All relationships do not neatly fit the above recapitulation. There is a minority of staff (River City) and students (Springfield) who adhere to alternative conceptions about how the occupational structure operates. The solution for one of these staff was to offer her resignation at the end of the year (the other staff member holding an alternate ideology has minimal connection with the day-to-day running of the program). In addition, several Springfield students do not passively accept the prevailing ideology that links success with schooling. This is likely related to the Springfield students' more marginal integration within the program as a whole. They respond by compartmentalizing OSRP as a job that one goes to a few hours a week to get paid.

The next three chapters will present some of the repercussions of this prevailing ideology upon the program's ability to provide its students with a curriculum that can meet its own objectives. Chapter 4 explains how the staff come to interpret their jobs within a program that essentially fails to achieve its goals. Chapter 5 focuses on the relationship between the staff and the parents, concluding that the program ideology encourages the former to make simplistic judgments about the latter. Chapter 6 highlights the relationships that OSRP students have with the schools. It is found that despite the fact that students and their parents have serious criticisms of the local schools, they share the same conservative ideology of hope as the program staff. They have no alternative language or context in which to comprehend critique.

4

Staff Perceptions

Chapter 3 examined the conservative ideology of hope that acts as a focus for OSRP. The ideology helps the staff and students interpret and perform their roles within the program. This chapter reports that the staff comprehend their work in OSRP in a manner rooted in this conservative ideology of hope. It explores the world of the staff as they interpret the program and its students. First, it examines staff views of the students themselves. The latter are perceived to be generally deficient in a number of ways: economically, emotionally, in terms of self-esteem, skill development, and so forth. Because of these problems, the students are seen as having three needs: authority, structure, and caring.

Second, the chapter explores the staff's interpretation of their own role within the program. Again, it is argued that their adherence to the program's conservative ideology of hope has repercussions for perception and action. The staff see some of their main roles as counseling students individually and in groups. Within these sessions, it is found that communications are carefully restricted: institutions are never questioned, and discussion of institutional barriers to upward mobility is silenced.

Last, the chapter examines the favorable view that the staff have of the program. They feel that they make a difference in their students' lives. This is done by reinterpreting key concepts such as "work" and "decision making." The staff look hard for and find examples where they think they have made a difference.

OSRP STUDENTS ARE DEFICIENT

The main view that the staff have of the students is that they have identifiable and significant deficits. Some of these are seen as being generally shared by all the young people within both groups, while others are viewed as being unique to individuals. These perceived weaknesses encourage the staff to view the students as having various needs: a craving for authority and the necessity of structure and caring.

OSRP personnel understand that their students are economically disadvantaged. This occurs as a matter of definition, since falling below the poverty line is a strict criterion for admission to the program. Related to this idea is an understanding that the students lack experiences that are consistent with a middle-class lifestyle. These perceptions help to explain the numerous "cultural" activities arranged by Gerald: for example, trips to the theater. From the staff's perspective, cultural events help to compensate for deficiencies originating in the home. Staff perceptions of family deficiency are clear in the following quotes:

Sally: They're all lacking in, you know, someone to care about them.

. . .

Gerald: I call his house at 10:30 at night, and he's not even home yet. I said, "Where the heck are you? You have school tomorrow." And then he's sleeping in classes and all this kind of stuff. And then there's no male role model in his house. His father's an alcoholic. He has no male role models like to help keep him accountable.

. . .

BH: So she hasn't experienced affection?
Jane: Oh no, not at all. Mother's a very, very large, overweight person who looks, she looks like she would be intelligent enough to speak with and that. But you get no eye contact, just an anger. Very, very angry face.

. . .

Kevin: Their home lives are unpredictable, full of cataclysms, unstructured.

. . .

BH: What are they at risk of?
Barbara: They're at risk of, um, becoming their parents, you know?

The River City staff agree that their predominantly African American students are suffering from low self-esteem. Louise puts it this way:

Louise: Although they might verbally say that they're great, their inability a lot of times to communicate or take part in things in a socially acceptable way, they show me they're not confident. They really do in fact not feel that good about themselves.

As the staff see things, River City's predominantly minority students are at considerable risk academically:

Gerald: The basic skills are dormant: ability to communicate well, ability to write well, and so on.

. . .

Louise: It's not just understanding what to do but they're lacking the skills on how to do it.
BH: Would that be true of all the students?
Louise: Pretty much all of the students.

. . .

Kevin: Well, they lack the resources from their backgrounds, from their lack of understanding of work. I try to communicate to them. Or they're caught up in themselves, their individualized dynamics. And they can't set those aside long enough to open themselves to increase opportunity for knowledge. You know, to exhibit a thirst for knowledge.

The River City and Springfield staff identify a plethora of residual deficits among their students. To cite just a few examples, Gerald repeatedly complains about the students' selfish nature, their inability to give to others or to the program when the occasion demands it. He disapproves of their repeated use of street language and inappropriate dress. Kevin remarks that these children are intolerant of adults, viewing them as the enemy. Louise talks of their physical and sexual aggressiveness with each other, of their loose sexual mores, and of the demeaning behavior that black males exhibit toward black females. At the Springfield site, Jane speaks in terms of personal characteristics possessed by various individuals: Terry and Judith are hostile, Brian exhibits signs of the same mental illness possessed by his parents, Patricia is a chronic liar and an operator, and Raquel is "special ed." She sees them as all being present oriented and peer oriented, and does not know if television is responsible for that.

In short, the staff view their students as being personally deficient in a number of ways. They are lacking in caring and/or proper supervision at home, in proper (middle-class) experiences, in a variety of skills, and in various personal attributes. According to the River City staff, this is partly linked to their lack of self-esteem. The staff use this interpretation to identify three main needs that the students have: authority, structure and caring. All are logically related to their perception of the students as flawed or defective. Consider the staff's views on the students' needs for authority and structure:

Gerald: You've got to offer something very structured for them to do. Very task-oriented. Then you have to make sure you give them positive reinforcement. . . . You know if you just give them something to do and don't say, "Hey, that's a good job. I like the way you did that," we're not making this a very effective experience.

. . .

Kevin: My maleness, my race, these remind them of positive and negative experiences. These kids will press you into being a disciplinarian, and that's not my style naturally. I ask, "Is this the way they want to be communicated with? Is this best?" But I feel unnatural and don't like it. Yet when I do it, they don't like it either because it reminds them of the dominant males they have experienced and don't like.

. . .

Louise: I think that was part of what was in play today when Obuagu spoke out because there was the structure there and it was all set up and they're not used to that.
BH: What do you mean, "they're not used to that"? Don't they get that in school?
Louise: Some of them never give in there either. Constantly sent out of the room, night after night detention. They may have more detentions than there are days in the year. . . . They're like constantly putting me to the test.

• • •

Jane: They're thinking that my advisory messages are, "Do it or else," rather than [suggestions]. And that's how they're taking it. "You do this or else" rather than, "Say, well, Mrs. H. said that. Let's follow her advice because she's been there." You know, and instead of that, they're thinking it's like, you know, punishment. So maybe that's their view of authority, you know. Maybe that's it.

Gerald and Louise appear to disagree with Jane and Kevin concerning the students' need for authority, but this disagreement nearly disappears upon closer consideration. Gerald and Louise see the students as lacking in authority in the home and/or at school: as a result, the program must provide structure on their behalf. Kevin and Jane agree that the students need structure, but they have ambiguous feelings about being "pushed" by the students to become authority figures in their lives. Both feel the young people pressuring them to enact that authoritarian role, sensing that this need originates within the students' backgrounds. Nevertheless, all four staff agree that an authoritarian relationship is somehow needed in relation to the youth in this program.

The staff members also agree that the students require caring. Gerald may call it "positive reinforcement," and Jane "camaraderie," but they concur with Sally when she says that these young people experience a lack of caring that must be addressed by the program:

Jane: Why do you think those kinds of kids do the smoking? That's a camaraderie. That's a real, you know, "Would you like one? Oh, wow, she's giving me a cigarette." Sure, those are all feelings that they don't get. Where else can they ask somebody for something and get a response like that?

• • •

Sally: I was just hearing it from the kids' point of view, which was, "Oh my God, nobody cares about me, and you know, I'm really messed up."

This issue of OSRP students being in need of caring will be discussed further in the next section. Here, I have tried to indicate the degree to which these staff define the students as being deficient in a variety of areas. Jane comes closest to defining them as "normal," but quickly articulates a long list of personal weaknesses that more than balances out her initially positive perceptions. The staff as a whole, then, view the students as needing a program such as OSRP that responds to their imperfections. Since the students are viewed as being in need of caring, the staff feel obligated to provide it for them. Since they either long for or need authority, this must be considered in deciding how to structure relationships. Let us now turn to an exploration of how the staff have come to interpret their own roles within OSRP.

INDIVIDUALIZED COUNSELING, IGNORING BARRIERS, AND SILENCING

As chapter 2 points out, OSRP staff see themselves as being responsible for giving their students career-related experiences within a caring, supportive environment that encourages them to aspire to and achieve middle-class status. Success is interpreted as something predictably achievable upon following the program's ideology. In this section, we will see that barriers such as class, race, gender, or track placement have no place in OSRP. The staff do not see any benefit in pointing out obstacles to their students. In fact, they think that doing so would only act to their students' detriment.

The staff agree that they should act as counselors to the students, helping them through their rocky days of adolescence. Consider one typical counseling session between Gerald and Wateef. Wateef has voluntarily come to him to seek advice concerning a problem that he is having in school:

Gerald excuses himself from the meeting [with Jane and Tim] and goes out in the hall to talk with Wateef. It seems that Wateef is in trouble at school (and about to be in more serious trouble) over revenge that he is about to take on another kid who "lied" about him and got him into trouble. Wateef swears to Gerald that he will do physical damage to this kid. Gerald responds with: "Here's how you look at the situation . . . . Don't be dumb . . . . Is this character worth it? . . . Are you better than he is? . . . Don't be a child . . . I'll be pissed off if you do something that gets you into trouble . . . . People of low self-esteem do things like this. Do you have low self-esteem?" Gerald then tells Wateef a story about himself and a previous boss. I hear Gerald say, "I was really upset, like you are now. I got emotional, but here's how I handled it . . . . You've got a reputation to maintain . . . . We're trying to teach you the best way to solve your problems. Coming to me is an important first step on your part." (field note)

After a phone conversation later that day with Gerald, I added the following to my field note: "Gerald feels that he talked him out of it by pulling out all the stops. He told him that if he is suspended, he will not go on the up-coming field trip, he will be out of the program, that he should not solve disputes by fighting, etc."

This form of counseling is not atypical of many of the sessions that I observed. The staff member is direct in his advice as to which are the correct and incorrect roads to follow. He sustains his arguments with a request for personal loyalty, demanding unquestioning support for officials such as school personnel. He threatens the student with punishments such as suspension from OSRP at the same time that he uses praise as a personal motivator.

By comparison, the two school counselors are more professional in how they exercise their role as counselor. Sally expresses her understanding of this role:

Well, part of it is having them feel good about themselves. You know, part of the whole healing thing about counseling is feeling that they're not so alone and feeling that other people are going through this and feeling that they're worthwhile. And that they're allowed to make a mistake and they're still not a bad person. And so empowering them would be to give them control of their own life and say, okay, so you had a crappy home life. You know, your dad drinks and he beats you up. And it's really crummy and you don't like coming to school, and you don't want to do this. But, your family is your family, God love them or hate them. But you got your future and how are you going to make yourself feel good? And let's find some good things about you that are gonna help you get out of this. And by demonstrating it in a group with the kids brave enough to say, "Hey look it, you know, I might come to school because my parents fought and I know I should have been here cause it's for me." That's empowering somebody and saying, you know, you're not really a victim. You really can take charge over this, and hopefully they'll get that support at least in a group setting and in a teaching setting.

There are differences between these two forms of counseling. The first approach has the counselor assume the role of the substitute parent by directing, threatening, and praising. The young person provides little input in how to solve his or her own problem. The second approach seeks to empower the students through their own communication with each other (within the group situation) or with the counselor (within the individual counseling situation). Empowerment is thought of as emanating from the student's understanding that problems are shared, not unique to individuals, as well as through the understanding that one has choice.

Both approaches, however, agree that solutions to problems are individualistic. Neither attempts to help the young person understand a framework within which to comprehend his or her problems as being related to social structures lying outside the individual. Institutions are taken as given, with solutions necessarily occurring within present structural arrangements. For example, Gerald did not question Wateef on the exact details of how the school officials handled the dispute between himself and the other youth. By not doing this, Gerald suggests that it is the student's misconduct that is of central concern, while the context in which it emerged and the school's response to the situation are only secondary. In fact, at no time did I see a staff member explore or question any school policies or practices with these youngsters, despite the weak and strained relations that many of the students have with their schools. Institutions are not questioned in these counseling sessions; they are accepted as fixed structures within which individuals must work to seek their goals and interests.

Most OSRP staff members genuinely believe in the benign nature of our social institutions. Some of the staff hold critical opinions about the social institutions around them (note the discussion in chapter 3 outlining the critical perceptions of Louise and Stanley). Yet they have decided that it is in the best interest of these young people to purposefully hide these critiques from them. Irrespective of personal viewpoint, the net effect in terms of programming remains the same: students meet a wall of silence and lack of support whenever they voice critiques of social institutions. For example, Jane talked to me of a casual conversation that she and some of the students were having concerning administrative policy changes within Springfield Senior High School, which recently tightened up its control. The students were voicing their opposition to such changes, calling the school "a prison" and claiming that they should be paid to go there. Here is Jane's retelling of her response to her students: "I gave them an adult opinion. You want to get paid? If you got paid for your work, Nick, you wouldn't have got two cents here, you know. And I'm saying, you know, your parents are paying tremendous amounts of money for you to get this education, and then you want more money on top of that? You know, you don't think of how the education's being paid." I asked Jane about whether OSRP should encourage its students to question the work world and to sometimes challenge its nature. Here is her response:

Jane: That's too much to ask. Just start on the basics. If they can accomplish the basics, it's great. To get them even being able to think about that [criticizing institutions], that's way over there. It's far too advanced.
BH: Should these kids be taught to accept institutions or to question them?
Jane: Thank you Bram. Questions we get in college. No, just, they can't. There's too many. They should be taught to question them, there's no doubt about that. But there are ways of going about it.

Tim is typical of the staff in his comments on this issue. His reasoning is that OSRP students recognize a class bias in the political system, but that the staff should not encourage that type of thinking:

They do blame society and their parents blame society on certain things, everything from the presidential election and how that shows more interest and concern on the upper class as opposed to the lower class. I'm not sure if that's, if I'd make that [criticism] a huge component of the program. . . . I think that I'd try to take that and turn it into some *positives* and see where we could go from there. Okay, we're stuck in this. Now how do we get out of this? Where do we want to be and where do we want to go and how do we get there? I think a lot of *negativisms* are not necessarily healthy and sometimes a lot of kids will use it as an excuse not to succeed. . . . Everybody can make it out if they talk to other people, if they have an earnest desire. I like to believe that. If I don't believe that, as a counselor I'm in trouble. (Emphasis added)

Other staff members concur with Tim in regard to the issue of student critique:

Stanley: There's *positive* ways you can expose kids to those, those underrepresentations. And I think that's what we need to do. We need to work for *positive* thinking instead of dwelling on the *negative* that exists. Because I think, given the state that most of these kids have to go home to every night, I don't want to dwell on that. (Emphasis added)

. . .

Allison: Yes, they have a right to be angry and dislike the system that they're a victim of. And no, because how long can you blame the system for your situation? If you use that as something to fall back on, you'll never get out of the cycle [of poverty]. (Allison is the secretary in Gerald's office.)

The staff feel, then, that it is in the best interest of the students to minimize the significance or importance of any real or perceived class barriers that exist in society. They recognize a distinction between being positive and negative. From the staff's perspective, their role is to be inspirational and positive about existing social institutions on the assumption that this represents their students' best chance to achieve upward mobility. The staff feel that if their students are encouraged or permitted to be negative and blame the system for their own failures, they will continue to do so to their own detriment.

Gerald and Kevin extend this analysis to the problem of racial discrimination. Their argument is consistent with the above perceptions about class: they ask OSRP students to ignore the existence of any real or perceived racial barriers. Blaming failure on racism is seen as being associated with more failure.

BH: Your sense then is that somewhere they've picked up this idea that blacks don't have the same opportunity to succeed in this country?
Kevin: I think that's true. They feel that way. But, they've learned it through reinforcement in any number of places. . . . Sometimes it's a convenient excuse to fall back on that old cliché, "Why should I go? I'm not gonna make it anyways." And after a while, it gets to the point where they just, it destroys their incentive, okay?
BH: So your job then is to try to break that way of thinking?
Kevin: Yes. Very much so. Yes.

. . .

BH: . . . I think what I'm hearing you say is that it does these young people no good to think about black people originally coming here as slaves and being oppressed by white people. Would you agree with that then? Is that what you're saying?
Gerald: These days and times, you know, people use those [negative ideas about race] as a crutch. A horrible crutch. That's "B.S.," you know. That's crap. . . . I don't, I don't like to look at, look at the past. We're not about that stuff. We're about what skills you're going to have that make you marketable for the future.

In sum, OSRP staff perceive that their best strategy for helping these adolescents is to minimize or ignore class and race (as well as other barriers and institutional imperfections). They see their role as helping these young people to acquire the attributes, skills, and motivations to succeed within the existing system.

SILENCING STUDENT "VOICE"

One of the ways that the staff enforce their perceptions of social institutions is by controlling the public flow of conversation within the program. Here is what Gerald has to say on this topic:

Gerald: But I wouldn't, I wouldn't sit still with that kind of comment unless I took that comment and rephrased it so it became a learning experience for everyone involved.
BH: So you wouldn't want it to just sit there as a negative thing?
Gerald: Right, exactly. And you have to do that. Because number one, we said it in our group that you talk about your opinion, but you don't say it in a manner that disregards or disrespects any part of the population. This, of course, is the rule. That means you've got

to think before you say, and our kids are, some of the kids just don't do that. So that means you've got to listen very carefully and make sure you are the moderator, *you have to control the discussion to make sure that what's received is totally positive.* (Emphasis added)

Young people, then, are seen as possessing positive and negative attitudes that must be controlled by the staff. If discussion becomes negative, Gerald sees the staff role as steering it back to a more positive track. He and Kevin recognize that negative ideas already exist out there within the lower class, African American community. They see these as ensuring future failure by acting as excuses or crutches. Instead, the staff refocus discussion along what they see as more positive lines that presumably better prepare the students for the future. Their perception is that there is no sense in dwelling upon the past or in criticizing social institutions, since this kind of thinking is beyond these young people.

OSRP staff view their role as helping to support their students within the parameters of their program motto: Success = Opportunity + Effort. While they recognize that this motto may be a simplification of reality, they believe that it is in the best interest of the young people they are attempting to serve. Cluttering up this image with institutional barriers such as those related to class and race only reinforce already existing negative ideas about how the stratification system works.

Two other barriers facing many of these young people have not been discussed: those related to gender or to tracking choices within schools. In these areas, I found staff attitudes to be consistent with those already expressed above. Tracking and gender are not thought of as issues worthy of discussion within the program, except in the most positive of ways. For example, it was never mentioned that fifteen-year-old Shalimar might experience obstacles to realizing her career objective of dermatologist, despite the fact that she is reading at a 3.9 grade equivalent level (according to a recent test score) and is achieving only mediocre grades within the nonacademic track of her high school. Somehow, the staff feel justified in simplifying for these young people, even when it is hard to understand how student hope can possibly overcome very significant barriers that are not being explicitly addressed.

STAFF EVALUATIONS OF OSRP SUCCESS

Despite certain limitations (many of which have already been discussed), the staff are surprisingly positive in their view of the program. With certain minor reservations, they see the program as providing an important and needed service to the community. They feel that OSRP properly meets those needs by having a positive effect upon its students. The staff express that they make a difference in students' lives, providing them with positive experiences that assist in their personal growth and development. This is accomplished by reinterpreting what success is and how it is to be calculated or determined. The staff interpret minor accomplishments as if they have disproportionate significance. There seems to be a need to make one's work purposeful and meaningful, even in the face of failure. Here is a sampling of staff evaluations of the program that I collected in response to the question, "Do you think OSRP is successful?"

Gerald: We got an A+ rating over the last two years. We are among the top three programs in the state. . . . This has been a positive year. . . . I think it's massively successful because we make a difference in a lot of these people. What we do is unique, exciting, and different. And when you work with special populations, that's what you want to do. . . . No one else is doing it in this county. Sometimes not even the state.

. . .

Stanley: The strengths are staff and expertise. . . . I really feel that we have a very, very, competent, committed, involved, concerned staff. Look at the level of professionalism. And when you get those dynamics working in a classroom environment, kids start feeling the respect, the love, the concern, and want to stay. And want to be productive. And I think it's the staff that encourages the kids.

. . .

Jane: To tell you the truth, the third year I thought it was just the best. I said, "Wow, it would be great to do this very same thing for the next two years!" . . . And we've just expanded twice each year after that. And added more and more and better and better.

These positive staff evaluations of the program are tempered by the more mixed reviews of Louise and Kevin. It will be recalled from chapter 3 that these two River City staff feel overpowered by Gerald's controlling nature. As a result, they have reservations about the implementation (not the goals) of the program. This eventually culminates in both of them submitting their resignations from the program at the end of the year:

BH: Do you think the program helps the kids feel more confident about themselves?
Louise: Yes. Just by virtue of the fact that they're interacting with some adults and they're associating themselves with the program that they hear is fantastic, the greatest thing in town. I hear them referring their friends for the same sort of reason: "You're really going to get a lot out of OSRP, you're going to enjoy it, you should sign up for it." . . . I think the program is a wonderful program but it has its problems that could be improved upon.

. . .

Kevin: On the whole, kids will benefit and I'm hoping that. I think one day it will burgeon. And when it burgeons, these kids and their behavior and everything that goes with it will come to fruition. And at that junction, at that moment in time, they will begin to see the kinds of men and women that we hope, ideally, that will serve us. . . . I think that they need our program more than they realize. I think later on, I think posterity will hold true. You know, I think it will be a testament. . . . But I'm saying here, you know, if they apply themselves to this program, they could get so much more out of it. And nothing is more frustrating than understanding that the kids derive almost a zero base benefit from participating in the program. I mean I want them to walk away with something, hold their heads high and say, "I went through OSRP and I got 100 percent out of that program. I completely invested myself and I got everything that OSRP had to offer."

BH: So these kids are not investing themselves in the program?
Kevin: No, not fully.

Louise and Kevin still maintain positive feelings about the program, but their comments lack the excitement and assurance of their colleagues. Louise talks about OSRP improving students' self-image because of their association with adults and with a program that the director touts as being "the best thing since sliced bread." On the other hand, Kevin is reduced to hope. He hopes that one day the students will look back and discover that the program has given them something worthwhile. He believes this, though, in the face of recognized student resistance that leaves them with "almost a zero base benefit from participating in the program."

Nevertheless, Louise and Kevin are a minority within OSRP. As a group, the staff express a number of reasons for believing in the program's effectiveness. They talk of their role in helping to develop the students' work ethic, their decision-making skills, and of making a difference in individual students' lives. Very often, under-standings of what is meant by terms such as "work" or "decision making" are stretched, allowing the staff to define program functioning in positive terms. Here are some of their responses to my question, "What kind of work ethic do you think the students have within the program?"

Barbara: Of course you're gonna have a blowoff day. Everyone does, you know? But there's days where they'll work for an hour straight and then they'll, you know, walk around and they'll joke around, you know? But the first half-hour is a blowoff. And the last half-hour is a blowoff. But if they can work for that hour, it's good, you know.

. . .

Jane: The majority of them, I think their work ethic is great. The accountability, the phone calls that we've taught them to make when they don't show. I think all of them are really super. And those that aren't, aren't here. Really, it was just one that couldn't conform to the rules. . . . So I think their work ethic is great. And I think what they've learned this year, they may not show it in the next ten years or so, but it's gonna come back to them. . . . And I believe there's relaxing time on a job. There's fun, there's conversation and that's what this is. This is an after-school job.

. . .

Kevin: Believe it or not, to these kids, I think hard work is manifested through showing up, through attendance, just being there. I think for some of these kids, they don't work at things, haven't been as strong as we would like. And I think in them rides the fact that they report on a consistent basis in the OSR Program. It relates to diligence and hard work, okay? Now we got to take them a step beyond that.

When I ask the staff about work habits, they provide answers that appear on the surface to be evasive. They respond to my questioning but do not discuss the actual difficulty, pacing, or style of the work that is done by the students within the program. I do not believe, however, that they are being intentionally evasive. This is the way they honestly interpret the work that goes on under their supervision. Their low opinion of these young people allows them to view such activities as showing up regularly and on time, being appropriately dressed, and phoning in when absent as "work." In a like manner, OSRP classroom time is considered to have been consistent with a good work ethic if only half of it is work related. In short, the staff do not chastise themselves for what I observed to be a startlingly relaxed work atmosphere (see chapter 2). Instead, they focus on the little strengths that they perceive in the students' behaviors. Then they blame whatever poor work ethic they do observe as being caused by character defects within the students themselves.

Gerald considers decision-making skills to be one of OSRP's most important focuses: "We give the kids a tremendous amount of responsibility so that we're challenging their ability to be able to think on their feet for a change. . . . There are many times I give the kids responsibilities." It is understandable that practice in decision making would be an important focus of this or any group that attempts to assist in the socialization of young people. After all, making decisions is an important part of everyday life for people of all ages. It makes sense to assume that one learns to make good choices through repeated trial and error. However, from my observations, I would agree with Barbara's assessment of the degree to which OSRP provides its students with regular opportunities to make decisions:

BH: Do you think that this program gives students help in making decisions?
Barbara: I think it will help them in the future, but I don't know about right now. Right now in the program a lot of decisions are being made for them. So they're not given a chance, you know. The only thing they make decisions on is what color construction paper their mini-project will be on or something. You know, everything else is like, "We've got to have this done, you don't have a choice." I'm hoping that once they get out into the job world they'll be able to make a decision.

The rest of the staff disagree with Barbara on this issue. They do not believe that the decisions that the students are asked to make within the program are limited. Nor do they say that this might be an area where they would like to see the program improved. Instead, like the issue of work, they reinterpret what it means to make a decision. Minimal decisions by students are elevated to a significant status. Sally is representative of the staff in her feelings about this issue:

BH: Does OSRP give the kids practice in decision making?
Sally: Uh-huh. One, deciding to come to the program. Two, they have to make decisions about being in class and having their attendance up or else they will not receive a pay check or they could be put on probation in our program. So that kind of forces them to be responsible for their decisions. They're looking at making choices as far as career stuff, which is all process. And they may decide, well, I'm not this and they learn about it. I want this. No, I want that. They're learning about making decisions when it comes to how to get along with others and to take responsibility for their actions.

According to Sally, one of the main choices that the program forces its students to make is whether or not they want the pay badly enough to attend school and OSRP on a regular basis. In addition, they are forced to make a decision (within the structure of the program) as to which career they want to do their research and their job trailing on. Third, Sally is arguing that they are making social decisions every day in choosing how to relate to others around them within the program. One cannot deny that these are, in fact, decisions that the students are faced with every day. But are these significant enough to articulate and take satisfaction in, such that the staff come away feeling that their program provides useful practice in decision-making skills? Or are they a reinterpretation of the banal and obvious, elevating them to an undeserved stature?

I did not observe significant, ongoing decision making within the program on a regular basis by anyone other than the staff. Every day the young people would observe the ritual of entering the classroom and socializing until staff decided to commence the day's work activities. Staff decide on what work is to be done, whether it is acceptable or unacceptable, and complete or incomplete. The students do decide things like their own attendance and pacing, and may face consequences in the form of a smaller pay check, adult disciplining, and/or suspension from the program. But these kinds of decisions are limited in that they involve minimal responsibility for individual action and no obligation to the collectivity.

Part of this staff agreement that students should only be involved in limited decision making comes from staff perceptions of the program and the students' place within it:

Jane: I constantly preach to them that *this is an employer-employee situation*, not school. (Emphasis added)

Just as Jane and Gerald make a point of repeatedly telling the students that they do what their bosses tell them to do, they expect their students to follow suit. A case in point is Gerald's response to my question about the suitability of a number of the job-trailing placements: "Whether they're bored to tears or whether they're very active to me is not very relevant." Staff present the ideology to students that employers direct and employees obey. This simple idea helps to explain the lack of decision making on the part of the students. Staff tell the students that when they become adults they will then have the authority to make decisions on behalf of others.

I observed above that the staff define these young people as deficient along a number of dimensions, including self-esteem, skill development, and various personal characteristics. I found no examples of staff articulating a relationship between holding negative perceptions and a reluctance to encourage decision-making activities (I doubt that any of the staff consciously understand that they in fact hold these negative opinions of their students). However, there is a logical relationship between holding such negative views and failing to plan activities that give them experience in handling choice and responsibility. It is easier to deny participation to a group that one defines (however malevolently) as losers than to do the same with a group of winners. Rosenthal and Jacobson (1968) have taught us that teachers' perceptions have a lot to do with how they subsequently react to and behave in relation to their students. By extension, it is likely that staff understandings of their students similarly influence programming, including the decision-making factor considered here.

One of the often-repeated themes of the staff is that "we have to measure success piece by piece with our students" (Gerald). They look for and report small signs that they are "making a difference" in the lives of these young people. This appears to be true even when the signs do not amount to anything more than a temporary improvement in a long, slow decline. Most of these examples of success are held out as evidence of the effectiveness of the program and/or the staff. Sometimes credit is taken for positive changes that occur in students' lives, even when the relationship between the changes and the program is tenuous at best. Interestingly, I did not hear staff members assume the responsibility for negative actions on the part of their students.

To cite a few examples, Gerald told me that he feels successful when he sees improvement in a student's dress or program attendance. He finds it significant when a young person approaches him with a concern that a mistake was made on his or her pay check. He tends to be very positive in his evaluation of how the students present themselves on field trips, making questionable claims about the experience's transferability to the classroom. One day, he told me proudly that Chalka had won the "student of the term" award in her special education high school:

Gerald: Anyway, I went back to that school in January and said, "Put this kid back in school, put her in an academic program cause she's doing fine." Last week, Chalka got student of the term. Honor role. I mean, that is a major accomplishment for her.
BH: So you feel that you're part of that, you've been successful along with her?
Gerald: Oh man, definitely.

There are a number of interesting aspects to this brief story. One is that the link between Chalka's success at school and Gerald or the program is a tenuous one. Second, Gerald unjustifiably jumps to the conclusion that student of the term means honor role.[1] Last, he does not put this event into the context of the large number of serious difficulties that Chalka has been having at school for many years. In fact, as things evolved, Chalka failed to complete her last term in school. This was related to her second pregnancy and to the family and emotional difficulties accompanying that circumstance. In short, this story reveals that Gerald is quick to glorify small achievements as being related to his own efforts, while he dismisses long-term difficulties as being out of his control.

Gerald is characteristic of the rest of the staff in this regard. For example, Tim feels successful for counseling a student to avoid his commitment to enter the military. He feels this way despite the fact that, unknown to him, the young man's mother was happy with his original decision and felt betrayed by the counselor. Similarly, Tim told me of the horrible job trailing he was having with Patricia (she was assigned to work for him in the high school counseling office twice a week). Yet, in the next breath he expressed the opinion that job trailing is a wonderful concept, and it should become an expanded part of the program. Jane takes credit for improving Leon's withdrawn personality because, after several months, he no longer "sits at a back table with a jacket over his head." Without a careful analysis, she erroneously interprets students' grades as going up, and attributes this to their need to bring their grade reports into the program. These staff analyses represent a general pattern of optimism, that is, of not looking for evidence that runs counter to their ideology of hope.

The staff find themselves in the position where they must search for and claim even remote signs of their own achievement. They personalize their contributions to the students in ways that allow them to feel that there is some benefit to their being there. They want to make a difference in the lives of these youth, and so they scrutinize events in order to validate that desire. Contradictory evidence is not actively sought to temporize or mediate many of their claims of success. Instead, it is put aside, thus allowing them to tolerate their situation. Clearly, their work must have meaning to them, and they will not accept failure as meaningful.

In this section, I have revealed the staff's positive evaluation of the program's success. Most mirror Gerald's enthusiasm and positive orientation to OSRP. They feel that the program is exciting and can make a difference in students' lives. They commit themselves to the program and care about its students. The main competencies that they see being taught include work skills and decision-making skills. It was found that they positively evaluate their ability to create situations in which these skills are effectively transferred by stretching the meanings that are commonly attached to words such as "work" and "decision making." This is facilitated by their belief that students have many personal deficiencies and by their definition of their relationship with students as being "employer-employee." Louise and Kevin appear to be exceptions to these general observations because of their unique relationship with Gerald. Yet, they agree that the program has a lot to offer its students. However, they are more restrained in their praise for the current program, preferring to think of it as having a dormant potential for success. Thus, despite the fact that the program fails to accomplish its own goals (chapter 2), the staff's inability to recognize or confront failure displays an inherent need to make their work meaningful by interpreting OSRP and their contributions to it in a positive manner.

CONCLUSION

Let us return to the unanswered question, "Are these findings related to the program's conservative ideology of hope?" I will briefly reconsider the main components of this doctrine. First, it optimistically accepts the view that society is open to all, irrespective of class, race, gender, and so forth. Second, it implicitly embraces the conservative position that institutions are properly regulated by a coherent and benign set of values and norms. Third, it suggests that upward mobility is achieved by working hard, by seizing opportunities, and by having hope. Those who fail to take advantage of society's open opportunity structure are viewed within this ideology as being deficient.

The findings of this chapter are congruent with the above set of ideas. First, the fact that the staff perceive OSRP students as defective is consistent with the segment of the ideology identifying failures as deficient. Since the program's purpose is to serve the needs of society's potential failures, it legitimates a view that those with power have the authority to integrate and control others who are marginal and/or defective. Second, the idea of individual counseling toward successful integration and upward mobility is premised on the supposition that our society is benign and open to upward mobility from all groups. An alternative explanation that I reject is that the staff purposefully deceive these young people by lying to them about the nature of our system of stratification. One must assume that the staff are well-meaning individuals who believe in the truth of their own ideological rhetoric. Third, the staff deliberately deliver the message that barriers do not exist for marginal people. This is consistent with the optimistic ideology of America being an open society, that is, of equality of opportunity existing for all. Finally, the data support the idea that the staff are essentially self-congratulatory in their understanding of their own contributions to their students. This is consistent with the hope aspect of their beliefs. It is a response of optimism, of believing that things will work out in the end and that staff have a part in creating a more societally acceptable finished product.

The next chapter will focus on the relationship between OSRP staff and the students' parents. Even though they do not often meet in face-to-face interaction, the staff develop conceptions about the parents that are based on their conservative ideology of hope. This acts to shape those relations in predictable ways that are sometime fraught with misunderstanding.

NOTE

1. In speaking with Chalka's school, I was informed that quite apart from progress in academic achievement, an improvement in student "behavior" could also be a basis for this award.

5

Contradictory Relationships
with Parents

This chapter examines the relationships that both OSRP staff and the students have with the students' parents. The staff were found to develop very definite conceptions of the parents, based on their observations of and relations with the students during program hours, and their limited face-to-face and telephone interactions with the parents themselves. OSRP staff perceive the parents to be deficient along a number of dimensions, despite the fact that there is contradictory evidence concerning the kinds of relationships that exist between students and their parents. This chapter also explores the students' perceptions of their parents, indicating that there is a wide range of parent-child relationships that defy simplistic generalizations. It is found that the staff's tendency to negatively evaluate and label the parents allows and even encourages them to show that they care for their students by adopting a "substitute parent" role with respect to OSRP students. This show of caring does not come without a cost. It is associated with conflict between staff and parents and with student resistance. I conclude the chapter by suggesting that the staff's negative perceptions of parents has its origin in the program's conservative ideology of hope.

DEFICIENT PARENTS

As I noted in chapter 4, OSRP staff perceive their students to be at risk because of their personal inadequacies. There are a number of possible competing explanations to explain the origin of this situation, but the staff have chosen the one that best complements their conservative ideology of hope. Since our system of stratification is viewed as being open and benign, some group or institution must be held responsible for the students' failure to achieve success at school. Within this framework, the nearest and most available group to blame is the parents. In a word, the staff find them to be deficient. This section will more closely explore the staff's thinking on this issue. It is surprisingly consistent, varying little from staff member to staff member. Since Gerald and Jane have the most contact with the parents and had a lot to say to me on this issue, I will allow them to speak on behalf of the other staff. Before turning to Jane's comments, let us consider some of the perceptions that Gerald shared with me concerning the parents:

You've got an at-risk child, you've got at-risk parents. Sometimes even more so. . . . I've got a lot of parents who've lost control with their children. You know, over and over again. I've got parents who are not assertive because they're at-risk themselves. . . . Parents don't communicate well with their kids. . . . [A student's] mother works a late shift and refused to change it. I said to her, "I think you should be home with him." Now his negative behavior is perpetuated by his mother. And she refused to change her schedule because she puts herself first, you know. That kind of scenario. . . . Because she's pregnant, at sixteen. With a very dysfunctional family. They're migrants, they travel all over the place. . . . Hakim's mother was incarcerated and so was Wateef's mother. . . . His father's an alcoholic. He has no male role models to help keep him accountable. . . . His home life is a complete disaster. There's no support at home whatsoever.

Gerald sees students' families as being dysfunctional in various ways and for diverse reasons. His most recurring theme is that the parents are not assertive enough to control their children. He explains this in a number of different ways—they are not strong enough, they are absent because of selfishness or incarceration, or they do not communicate well enough. He reasons that his students are at risk because of their parents. This is frustrating to him because he feels that he cannot adequately do his job without the proper support of parents. When Jane looks at her group of parents, she sees similar though not identical problems:

Father alcoholic, mother schizophrenic. No rewards ever and getting quieter and quieter, losing it every day. Just because there was nothing in it for him any more. . . . She comes in and attacks. It's all defensive. I hate that. As negative as you can be. She goads and lies. And it's so hard on Patricia that Patricia has become a liar because of it. Patricia is being tortured by her mother. . . . There's a mental torture that I think sometimes is often worse than a physical torture. . . . Because she's alone raising a family—the husband's in prison. And she's just a really tough hard abrasive human being. . . . Another situation is when they have so little at home. The motivation is lacking there and also they become at-risk when parents don't make a big fuss about anything they do wrong. . . . They don't know how to draw a line and say this is not acceptable. . . . They see their parents getting along with so little. And they come home and they can eat and put their feet up and watch television. And they're happy and they can be lazy and they can be contented. . . . Why should they care about an extension of their life, you know? They're tired. They're as lazy as the previous generation because their parents did the same thing—showed them how little they can get by on and that's it.

Rather than focusing on one theme, Jane describes a variety of personality deficiencies among her students' parents. In addition to agreeing with Gerald's concern about parents lacking control over their children, they are also seen as alcoholic, mentally ill, passive, incommunicative, liars, lazy, and contented with so little. She argues that children raised by such parents are victims, thus satisfying her desire for an explanation of their at-risk state.

Jane goes beyond these personality deficiencies, however, to attack the parents for "milking" the welfare system. Any sympathy that might have been detected above gets completely abandoned when money is discussed:

Jane: We've had parents who have nursed their medical situations: backs and legs and bones. They've nursed it and nursed it. "And I can get this check and I don't have to do diddley squat." You know? . . . I asked [a former OSRP student], "Why did you ever quit school? You had everything going for you. You were smart, you were hangin' in there, and you were doing well." And he says, "What difference does it make? I get $400 a month until I'm twenty-one anyways and I've always had that. That's been my money." And I said, "Oh really, and why is this?" He said, "Oh I had that Legg-Perthes disease a long time ago." And I said, "But that's healed now. My daughter had Legg-Perthes disease when she was nine years old. . . . There's all different therapy and that." And he says, "Hey, my mother knows how to manipulate things."

BH: He got some kind of a settlement from an insurance company?
Jane: Disability. Yes, disability. He has a limp or something. I never noticed it in five years.
BH: So you feel that acts as a disincentive for him to be responsible?
Jane: Sure. Sure.

Jane senses abuse of her tax and/or insurance payments, leading to an anger on her part toward these parents. They are no longer just deficient in personality. Instead, they are involved in a variety of financial schemes verging on fraud. What adds insult to injury for Jane is that this parental behavior sets a negative example for their children. They learn from their families that they can benefit from doing "diddley squat." And so the cycle of welfare is passed on from generation to generation.

The staff are agreed then, that the parents are to blame for the at-risk school status of their children. They assume this position, however, despite contradictory evidence concerning the ties between these parents and their children. In my interviews with the students, we discussed their relations with their parents. What emerged was a complex and contradictory image of these relationships that goes well beyond the simplifications outlined above by the staff. The students were able to point out a variety of "hurts" that they experienced in relating with their parents. At the same time, however, other pictures emerged: images of warmth, caring, guidance, and protectiveness. I will present these two contrasting views of parents, as seen through OSRP students' eyes.

PARENTAL HURTS

There is evidence upon which the staff or any observer could make severe judgments of some parents. However, the students have a different point of view from the staff, and this shows up when they evaluate their parents for their shortcomings. Unlike the staff, they never talk of parental laziness, welfare fraud, or an inability to control their children. Instead, they criticize their parents for four main types of abuse: substance abuse, psychological abuse and neglect, physical abuse, and sexual abuse. I will briefly present fragments of discussion with the students in each of these areas.

Substance Abuse

Brian: Both my parents became alcoholics and my dad lost his job and decided that he could work at a variety store somewhere. He like dropped down. And my mom had her nervous breakdown.

. . .

Terry: My father died when I was six and from then on my mom moved around a lot. She had different boyfriends. . . . And she got involved with guys who were involved with drugs. And that's how she got herself in trouble.
BH: Did she end up in jail then?
Terry: Ya. . . . So that's how I ended up with foster care. First it was just the emergency phase, to see what was going to happen, but then when they realized she was going to be in there for a while, I was moved to [nearby city], and then I was moved down here.

. . .

Argina: My father and mother would be married for twenty-eight years and he just moved out in February of last year. He's an alcoholic. And so, my mother got tired of it. So she kicked him out the house and stuff.
BH: Do you still see him?
Argina: Ya, he still come over to my house. He want, he want to move back in, but my mother, she won't let him. Cause he's been stealing her stuff, stealing my stuff, stealing everybody . . .

Psychological Abuse/Neglect

Quionna: She [my grandmother] said my mother would, she would pick me up from off the floor and go put me in a crib. You know, just let me, you know, in a dark room and let me cry. And stuff like that. And I didn't, I didn't like that. . . . Like if my mother, if she needs some money or something, if I don't have it and I say, "Well mom, I don't have it right now." She goes, "You're lying. You don't, you just don't want to give it to me" or something like that. And I just hang up in her face. And then she'll call back, "Don't you hang up in my face. I'm your mother. I brung you in this world and I take you out of it." And I'm like, "How you gonna do that to me?" And that gets me real upset.
BH: So your mom hasn't done much over the years to kind of prove herself to you?
Quionna: No, she hasn't done nothing.

. . .

Andy: He's [my dad's] been around off and on. Like we would go to his house like every other week for like six months or something like that and then we wouldn't hear from him for a year. Even when we were over at his house like this weekend, we went Thursday, Friday, Saturday, Sunday, and Monday. He said maybe two words to me the whole weekend. It's not like we're going to visit him, we're going to visit our step-mother, really.
BH: He is a person who has let you down?

Andy: Ya.

BH: And that's hard for you?

Andy: Ya. He never really did like any of the things like kid stuff with us. He never threw the football or played frisbee or nothin' like that.

. . .

Louis: It's like once a year kind of thing I talk to him. . . . I do care about him and stuff but he don't talk that much. . . . It's like I feel kind of ignored by him, because, you know, he never calls or nothin'. So . . .

Physical Abuse

Eric: My dad use to baby-sit me. But I guess he use to beat me for no reason cause I remember hiding behind chairs and stuff whenever he came and he'd be looking for me. My ma said that's because he always use to beat me.

. . .

Patricia: I used to get discipline after discipline [at school], and my mom would never find out about it.

BH: The school would never tell her?

Patricia: Ya. Cause they knew what she would do. Because of all the past things that she's done to me. . . . She'd find out and she'd beat the crap out of me.

BH: So that creates a problem in your relationship with her?

Patricia: Well, I can't trust her any more and it's like she, I don't consider her as my mom, you know?

BH: So that really leaves you on your own?

Patricia: Exactly, where I want to be.

. . .

Andy: When I was real little, about five or six, she used to be abusive. So we reported her to the child protective. And just this summer she was like not physically abusing me but abusing us by keeping us in the house and stuff like that. So me and my brother, we ran away to my grandpa's house and we reported her and she got psychiatric help.

Sexual Abuse

Maria: Well the problem really was that they thought I had had sex before. I did, with one of my, well, my uncle. He was molesting me, I guess you could call it.

BH: Why did you run away?

Maria: Because my mom was really just getting to me and I needed time away from them. Plus my mom said that she was going to tell my dad. Cause I told her many of my uncles had molested me. And I told her who and she said, "Well, I'm gonna have to tell your dad." You know, I was really panicking. I didn't want him to know. So I ran away. And I figured, you know, I can trust my dad. And he said it was all my fault, you know, cause I didn't say anything.

. . .

Argina: I think that's the reason why, part of the reason why, you know, I didn't get good grades then cause, you know. Plus I was molested at one time. So I think that's all part of the reasons why I was doing bad in school. . . . I think my teacher knew because when I was in the third grade, you know, I went out to, went to gym to go play. She had me stay in and she talked to me, she told me she was molested at one time too. And she asked me had that ever happened to me. So I told her, "Ya." So then they called in my father and all that and then my teacher told me to tell my mother. So I told my mother all that stuff. Then they took me to the hospital to see did he enter inside me. But no he didn't. So my mother asked me all what happened and stuff.

These parental deficiencies are important and real to the students. I am sure there were others who did not trust me enough to confide in me at this level of intimacy. It seems likely that OSRP youngsters, as a group, have experienced more than their share of abuse from adults around them. It is not hard to imagine that these circumstances have indeed affected them profoundly in their relationships with others, with social institutions, and with themselves.

However, it is important to point out that these students' critiques of their parents are very different from those of the staff. According to the staff, the parents are lazy, uncaring, passive/uncontrolling, and fraudulent. The students, on the other hand, view them largely as abusive in one form or another. Some of this discrepancy can be accounted for by the fact that the students do not readily share this kind of personal information with adults who enter and leave their lives on a regular basis (such as school teachers, guidance counselors, and OSRP staff members).[1] As well, part of the difference between these two groups' perspectives may be accounted for by the fact that they approach the parents from different points of view. One group is strongly emotionally involved and often dependent financially, while the other is examining them from a more distant, middle-class perspective that accepts certain ideological presuppositions (previously discussed).

Why is this distinction between staff and student perceptions significant—after all, both are views of deficient parents? What difference does it make if the parents are viewed as having one or another set of defects? It seems that perceptions of others are necessarily based on fragmented information. In the absence of full knowledge of the other, we rely on our ability to interpret the segments that we are exposed to. By necessity, these are filtered through our ideological lenses, selecting from and adding meaning to the information received. OSRP staff see the parents as deficient in ways that are systematically different from the students' perceptions. This shows that when a full view is not available, people will content themselves with a partial one that can be interpreted from the perspective of their implicit ideology (in this case, the conservative ideology of hope). This discrepancy between images becomes even more significant when we add our finding that many OSRP parents are fulfilling their role in ways that are consistent with love and caring. Although the above hurts and injustices cannot be minimized, it is necessary to also recognize the positive relationships that exist between OSRP students and their parents. For the staff, there is no differentiation: they lump all the parents together as deficient.

PARENTAL ASSISTANCE AND ENCOURAGEMENT

The above findings of parental hurts are only one component of the multifaceted relationships between students and their parents. There is also evidence of several very close, caring, and concerned links between parents and children. What follows is a series of segments from student interviews about these more positive connections. For clarity of presentation, I have divided them into sections that discuss relationships, academic goals, and protectiveness. These were the three most often-repeated themes emerging from the interviews.

Parent-Child Relationships

Quionna: I love my grandmother. Like, I call her mom, cause I been living with her for so long. She, you know, she talk to me, you know. She take me and she talk to me and everything. And we go church every now and then. They go Sunday, Sunday nights, Wednesday nights, and Friday nights. And I go with her sometimes, you know. You know we talk a lot.

BH: And what about your grandfather? What kind of relationship do you have with him?

Quionna: I like my grandfather and I like to go fishing with him in the summer. It's like my grandfather and I, we always pals. Like as if I was his son or something. I like to go hunting and fishing and stuff.

. . .

Latoya: I think I see eye to eye with my mother about mostly everything. My mother, we're like sisters. She's like my older sister, that's just how close we are. But sometimes we have different problems like if I want to go somewhere I tell her I'll be back at one time, she'll tell me another time. Well I disagree, but of course I have to follow her time, but you know we disagree. Because the other night my friend asked me to come over and I told her I'd be back at 11:30 and she wanted me home at 11. I really didn't see the difference between a half an hour because she knew exactly where I was at. But I guess she knows what's best so I just came home at 11.

BH: So you don't get into the habit of arguing with her about that half-hour, you tend to agree?

Latoya: Uh huh. Because I was always taught not to talk back to older people. You know when someone older tells you to do one thing, you don't disagree, you just do it, you know, not arguing.

BH: So you don't have any basic disagreements.

Latoya: We don't have any, you know, real arguments where I don't even talk to her or whatever because I know from different situations and past experiences that I know that I'm goin' to always need my mother. No matter what happens, she's always going to be there. And so there's no reason to argue because I'm always going to have to come back to her for something.

. . .

Felicia: My parents gave me a lot of support on that. They was just always bragging about me. They was always bragging about me, my grandmother used to always hug and kiss me. And you know, everything like that.

· · ·

Early: I feel close to them, but my father, I feel closer to him. I be hanging with him a lot.
BH: Where do you see eye to eye with your dad?
Early: He do things that I like, like work on cars and stuff like that.
BH: Does he let you work alongside him?
Early: Yes. Where he would tell me, you know work with him. Do, just do it. Or I just do it for him without him asking.

Academic Goals

Latoya: My mother always, she always expressed, "Go to school" and, you know, "Get good grades so you can be something." And my father, too, because when he was little, he lived in Georgia and they didn't really have to go to school. So he didn't go and he didn't graduate. So he taught me and my brother that he wants us, you know, to learn how to read and write and all that and graduate.

· · ·

BH: What does he want for you?
Brian: High, high grades. And, I don't know, just really, just to do well.
BH: Why does he want that?
Brian: I'm really not sure. Probably cause he didn't do very well and he wants me to do well.

· · ·

Leon: My dad, he's fair. He's strict, but it's the right thing to do because when we come home all we want to do is sit down and play Nintendo. And right now, I've gotten low grades, because I don't do my homework, but my dad took the Nintendo away. So the grades are coming up. And if we get below a 75, we get grounded until the progress reports come out, to tell us we're doing better. . . .
BH: Where do you see eye to eye? Where do you kind of agree with them about things?
Leon: Doing homework before going out to play. Because if I hold off, like on Fridays I think I've got the weekend to do it and they go, "No, do your homework first and then you go out and play." I think it's fair. If you hold off too long then it becomes Sunday night and you don't got your homework done.

Parental Protectiveness

LaKesia: My mom, she don't allow us to go out like say like to go to a party. If she do we got to be back at 12. Party start at 10. That ain't no time. If a boy want to take us to the movies, she want to go with us (laughs).
BH: Why do you think your mom is so strict with you?
LaKesia: She don't want us to end up like she did. She had us, she had my two sisters when she was in high school and she was about to have me when she was graduating.

• • •

Felicia: They, well they just want us to stay, they just don't want us go get into any kind trouble. They just, like they don't want us going out in the streets and, especially, they don't like us going out, they don't want us going into the street and getting hurt. They don't want us to do nothing stupid.

• • •

BH: So do they try to keep tabs on where you are and where you're going?

Joyce: All the time, "Where you going? Who you going with? What time you planning on being back? How are you getting there? How are you getting home?"

BH: And how do you react to all that questioning?

Joyce: I mean, I can see they're concerned, but sometimes it just drives me up the wall. They're like, if I tell them I'm going with somebody I usually don't hang around with, they're like, "Well, I want to meet this person first." And when I first started hanging around with Frank, my dad like, "Well, I want to meet him before you go out driving with him."

BH: So what's their concern? What are they watching over you for?

Joyce: Just to make sure I don't get in trouble I think. And you know, so that nothing happens to me.

BH: Are they worried about rape or sexual assault or . . .

Joyce: I don't know, maybe. My mom's always worried about stuff like that. She's like, "Don't go walking or don't go home from May's house by yourself." She's like really worried about that. . . . And they're always worried, like, "Well make sure whoever you're driving with isn't drinking."

These interview segments show that the staff hold selectively distorted perceptions of the parents. Their focus on one set of parental deficiencies to the exclusion of other complexities is startling. It seems that they accomplish this by selectively interpreting fragments of information that are immediately available to them, according to their preferred ideology. When they are able to successfully integrate this information, they simply stop seeking (or cease listening to) new information that might contradict these understandings. Put another way, it appears that if the staff look hard enough, they are able to find confirmation for their supposition that these children are at risk because their parents are unworthy. The above data show that the staff's negative stereotypes are oversimplifications of how the parents feel about and relate to their youngsters. Many of the parent-child relationships are warm and caring on both sides, characterized by compromise and understanding. Academic goals are often stressed, with several parents hoping that their children will succeed where they themselves failed. There is a pattern of parental protectiveness (particularly of females) that reveals fears of violence, sexual assault, drugs, alcohol, early pregnancy, and so forth. These data largely refute the staff generalization that OSRP parents are apathetic about their children's progress in school and unconcerned about properly supervising or disciplining them. This negative stereotyping, however, remains intact. In the next section, I will suggest that the staff's negative perceptions are used as a legitimation for assuming a substitute parent role with respect to the students.

THE STAFF AS SUBSTITUTE PARENTS

At the beginning of this chapter, it was revealed that the staff are unanimous in their feeling that the parents are deficient. Because the staff sense their own relative superiority, they feel that they have the right to parent "in partnership" with the students' real parents. Jane expresses this feeling of staff superiority: "I used to be a bleeding heart and every day come home to my husband and say, 'If I could just get that one in this household for a little bit. Just get them here, you know.'" Implicit in the above statement is Jane's understanding that her and her husband's expertise as parents stands in contrast to the student's parents' deficiencies, and that this would make a world of difference to the child being referred to. Because she views herself as being able to provide a "better" home than the parents, she feels free to step in and assume a substitute or co-parenting role herself. Other staff express this type of thinking in the following interview segments:

Gerald: I reinforce the idea that we're partners in your child's success. The only way this student is going to make it . . . throughout life is with us together. . . . They have to be partners with me.

. . .

Kevin: As far as being surrogate parents, yes, in some regards I think that's true. I would like to be in some positive way. . . . That's almost the nature of the program by the nature of the beast.

. . .

BH: You see the program in a way as sort of a substitute parent?
Tim: In a way, yes. Ya, I think it is. At least the way our career educator at Springfield sees it. She likes the program I think very much. They act like a parent to these kids.

. . .

BH: Are you a substitute parent? Is that what you're doing in that group?
Jane: Exactly. Exactly, and that's what I think the teacher's role should actually be. And not many people are willing, because it takes an awful lot out of you. Parenting takes a lot out of you. . . . [I'm the] mother who pushes and gets upset when they don't do things. And isn't upset when I'm put down cause I don't get bent out of shape, you know. I don't take it personally cause I know kids. But, nagging and the harping and the yelling and the reminding, constant reminding and all that, you know.

The staff see themselves as picking up where the parents leave off. They offer advice that they perceive the parents are unable or unwilling to do: disallowing street talk and disheveled dress, acting as a role model worth following, offering wisdom, pushing, nagging, and so forth. Because the parents are viewed as inadequate, the staff take what otherwise might be considered to be inappropriate liberties with the children. In contrast, they view themselves as going the extra distance by assuming this substitute parent role.

Some staff argue that they should not be limited to co-parenting the students. They believe that OSRP (and/or some other social agency) should reach out and control the parents. Jane expresses this view in her opinion that there is a need for parents to be adequately schooled in parenting: "I believe that a parent or pre-parent should have mandatory schooling. Mandatory for the first five years of the child's life. I'm absolutely convinced of it. And schooling to the point where they can watch things happening and interaction between the child and the mother, and be able to say, 'Look, what you're doing with that child right now is wrong.'" Gerald echoes this lack of faith in these at-risk parents by suggesting that they need to be controlled as an inherent part of OSRP:

We know what's happening with these parents. . . . I want to be able to say to the parent, "You either help us or your child is out of the program." The parents have got to be helped to understand that nine to twelve hours a week is a big new time commitment for these kids. . . . The parents will also need counseling. . . . I want the parents to have a mirror program. They must make meetings, have a parent advisory board, be encouraged to attend field trips. This gets the parents proactively involved rather than reactively involved. . . . We want more guidance [to the parents] on how the money from the program will be spent. We want parents to agree on a guideline. I will ask the parents, "How are you going to communicate with your kid on how to spend the money?" (Field note)

These data indicate that the two senior program staff seek to penetrate further into the parental domain. Jane wants to impose expert parenting conceptions upon these at-risk parents through a mandatory education program teaching middle class parenting practices. Gerald seeks to extend the program's control over the parents in a variety of areas that concern him. For example, he does not perceive the parents as adults who have had experience in spending money over a number of years.

In sum, the staff feel completely justified in extending their understanding of their role to include "parenting." The two senior staff want to control how these parents carry out their parenting functions either directly through the program (Gerald), or indirectly by means of mandatory parenting classes (Jane). It seems likely that these ideas originate in the staff's less than complimentary view of the parents. These suggestions come dangerously close to a kind of colonization of the lower class by the middle class. The latter perceive the former as deviating from accepted patterns of thinking and behaving. As such, poor parents are thought to be in need of remediation in order to adequately socialize themselves to meet middle-class standards. In the following section, it will be shown that conflict between staff and parents is the inevitable result of this pattern of thinking.

CONFLICT OVER CARING

Because of the staff's perception of the students and their parents as being deficient, they seek to care about the whole child. The structure of the program seems conducive to the carrying out of this goal: the low student-staff ratio encourages flexibility and individual attention; the small number of students in the program permits a sense of intimacy; the program is noncompetitive, having no grades that could interfere with a caring relationship; and the staff pride themselves in being able to respond to the needs of the whole child, valuing counseling as an appropriate response to help their students through individual difficulties. This idea of a concerned, caring staff is repeatedly voiced by those related to the program: parents, students, work study placement personnel, and so forth. Stanley (the principal administrator) sums up what I found to be a consensus on this issue: "The strengths [of OSRP] are staff and expertise . . . I really feel that we have a very, very, competent, committed, involved, concerned staff. Look at the level of professionalism . . . . And when you get those dynamics working in a classroom environment, kids start feeling the respect, the love, the concern, and want to stay. And want to be productive. And I think it's the staff that encourages the kids." Kevin described his co-worker Louise to me in the following terms: "She has a closer kinship with them [the students] than the teachers at school. She communicates marvelously, is attuned to subtlety, cares, is committed." In one of my discussions with Gerald, he revealed the following to me (as recorded in my field notes): "Gerald told me that he was only recently informed of the fact that a student in the program dropped out of school in December. When he found out about it, he acted swiftly to contact the boy's home, ended up waiting there until 3:00 A.M., talking with him, and getting him back into school." Gerald and Louise are not unlike the other staff members whom I observed in OSRP. They show a willingness to donate their time to guide their students through crisis situations, to advise or counsel them, and to contact institutions and advocate on their behalf. Since the staff define themselves as being "committed," "concerned," and "caring," and my observations concur with those assessments in some respects, it would appear that OSRP might be an appropriate context in which to observe caring in action. The context has already been described above as one in which the staff are inclined to blame the students and their parents for their deficiencies. This gives the staff the feeling that they have the right and the duty to act as substitute parents on behalf of their students. They feel that since the parents are primarily to blame for their children's deficiencies, their parental role can be infringed upon whenever they deem it to be in the best interest of the child. From the perspective of OSRP staff, their substitute parenting is a logical extension of their caring role.

OSRP's caring model is best illustrated by the detailed discussion of one situation that exemplifies my findings. The following narrative represents a type of relationship between staff and parents that I found to exist in a number of cases. Despite the context of caring, these relations are often characterized by anger, misunderstanding, lack of communication, and blame. They are the result of a staff who have such a low opinion of their students' parents that they feel entitled to step in and take over that caring, parental role when they believe the situation merits it.

Jen is a fifteen-year-old high school sophomore attending the Springfield program under Mrs. H.'s leadership. For the last few months her attendance at OSRP has been sporadic, due to medical problems. It seems that these may be related to a fire that killed a little girl whom Jen had baby-sat for for approximately three years. Consider her mother's understanding of this situation:

Mrs. H. just kept saying that I was making excuses for Jen, you know, on her illness and different things. But when Nova died in that fire, Jen went through a lot. I spent nights with her crying, you know. And Mrs. H. says, "Well, she can't dwell on that." Maybe some people look at things in one direction, you know. But I don't take it against Jen for feeling the way she did. She baby-sat that little kid since she was six weeks old, and she was three when she was burned in the fire. I mean Jen is a loving person. Jen is one when she gets attached to you, she's there. But when I talked to her. . . . she just kept saying I was making excuses for Jen. She works with teenagers. Doesn't she understand they have a hard time in life anyways, not putting extra situations in there? But yet you cannot just say to this child, "Go do what you have to do and put that out of your mind." I mean this is what she was telling Jen, "When you go to work [at OSRP] you have to go to work and you have to do." But you have to understand, she's also trying to grow up. And being a teenager is hard enough. Yes, I agree, I should make Jen grow up and learn and that's what I try to do. But there also you have to have some understanding.

The basic confrontation here is between a mother who is making excuses for her daughter and a staff member who feels that it is in a student's best interest to leave her personal problems behind when she goes to work (at OSRP). They disagree about which approach is most appropriate in this situation. As the story unravels, it will be clear that this and other discrepancies in viewpoint cause friction among the three people in this relationship. It seems that Mrs. H. has some concerns about Jen's general state of health, and these concerns eventually manifest themselves in her calling in the state's child protection agency. Jen's mother (who was caring enough to make excuses) suddenly becomes the opposite: a neglectful parent. Consider Mrs. H.'s point of view on this issue, as recorded in my field note:

Jen is not here (again). Mrs. H. tells me that this is Jen's week to receive more medical tests. She thinks that the mom is "neglectful" and threatens to file a child abuse report. Mrs. H. tells me that her own daughter was diagnosed with cancer at age nine, and that this was her worst experience as a mother. She feels that because Jen was told two or three months ago that an immediate operation is needed that might diagnose cancer, failing to act has gone on long enough. Mrs. H. told me that she had referred the family to a "charity" clinic, and her mother's reaction was something like, "We are already on a waiting list there." Mrs. H. told me that she would take the child abuse report forms home, fill them out and submit them tomorrow. She said that her relationship with Jen would not be jeopardized because the child abuse reports are guaranteed to be anonymous.

Instead of perceiving Jen's mother as caring enough to make excuses for her daughter, Mrs. H. now sees this woman as being cold and insensitive to the point of permitting her daughter to go for months without a needed operation that might diagnose cancer. Mrs. H. sees herself as the only person caring enough about Jen's health to represent her best interests. Consider the mother's point of view on the topic of her daughter's health care, as well as her reaction to Mrs. H.'s handling of the situation:

Jen's mom: And Mrs. H., she'd just say to me, "Well you don't care." I do care. It's just that I, I work. I've got a lady friend that's my, she's been like a mother to me, that's been ill. I've been trying to take care of her, cause her daughter works the four to twelve shifts and you know, it's. Ya, I know I should spend time with my kids but I know she's in good hands [staying with her older sister during the week].
BH: So in a way you feel like you were unfairly judged by Mrs. H.?

JM: Yes I do. And she would not listen to nothing . . . . I mean you cannot, you have to listen to a person too, you can't judge them before you hear. How can I say it? You can't be, you know. She just, she just had her mind made up: this is what it was and this is and you know and this is what you're doing. And she was making it worse on Jen, you know. And it wasn't helping the problem. It was, to me, worsening. And she just aggravated me to no end. And I, I didn't think it was fair. I just feel that she's a very unfair person, that's all. And I don't like her taking it out on Jen. Ask the doctor, you know? She just, you know, I said I just could not send her for all the extra tests and the doctor we saw at the time did not feel, he felt it was, Jen was ah, too much, how do you put it, what did he call it, too much on her for, in her life, her body going through all the changes, and you know. And I tried to explain this to Mrs. H. You know I'm not one that can talk in all kinds of terms. I'm just a common, you know.

BH: So the problem is that Mrs. H. didn't accept your doctor's, or your understanding of your doctor's, explanation?

JM: Yes. And telling Jen, "If your mother doesn't do this and your mother doesn't do that." I mean, you can't tell a child that, I don't care what anybody says.

BH: So she was really putting her against her mother in a way.

JM: Ya. And you know that wasn't any good either. I just cannot believe that she could be that way at working with teenage kids.

This conversation with Jen's mom is revealing. It exposes a mother who feels that appropriate and sufficient medical attention is being received by her daughter. It discloses an anger that grows out of Mrs. H. not listening, being too quick to judge based on only partial evidence, setting daughter against mother, and so forth. It also reveals some feelings of powerlessness in confrontation with a middle-class state representative ("I'm not one that can talk in all kinds of terms. I'm just a common . . . "). In this regard, Jen largely agrees with her mom's view of things. Consider some of her comments related to this situation:

Jen: She [Mrs. H.] had no right to do what she did. You know, either call and talk to my mom and talk, find out from my mom what was going on. You know, not jump to conclusions. Because she lied to him [child protection worker], told him different stuff, you know, which was untrue. She had no right to tell him, as far as I'm concerned. As far as my mom, because, you know, my aunt, my uncle, my sister, my mom, everybody feels the same way. She shouldn't have done what she done.

BH: Did anybody say that to her?

Jen: You can't say it to her. She's right. . . . She had no business to do it. That got me and my mom fighting because my mom thought I made her do it and I said, "No, I didn't." I said, "She did it on her own." I says, "If she keeps up with it, I will quit OSRP because I'm not gonna put up with that. Because she doesn't have the right to do it."

BH: Why do you think she did that?

Jen: I don't know. Cause, she knows I've been getting medical attention and she told him [child protection worker] that I had no, I wasn't getting the proper medical attention that I needed for what was wrong. And that is a big lie because I told her the one day that I went there [to OSRP] to pick my check up, that I had just gotten back from the doctor's and I couldn't go to work because the doctor told me to go home and rest.

BH: So you can't understand her doing that?

Jen: No.

Jen sides with her mom in this confrontation. She sees her medical attention as being satisfactory, and simply cannot understand why Mrs. H. would lie to the child protection worker as she did. Her explanation for this misunderstanding is that Mrs. H. "jumped to conclusions" without talking to her mom.

This narrative reveals that communication between staff, students, and parents is far from complete. Even though the participants do not express themselves using the concept of "social class," it appears that the parent in this case senses a middle-class arrogance and control, while the staff member interprets a lower-class incompetence and uncaring attitude toward the child. The lower-class mother does not feel that she is able to communicate on an equal footing with the middle-class staff member, while the latter feels that the former is being deliberately evasive in her communications. The dynamics of this relationship, including the crossing of class barriers, certainly adds a dimension of unpredictability and potential misunderstanding.

The above story exemplifies a student and parent reaction to a caring OSRP staff member. The use of the term "caring staff member" may seem like a contradiction in the sense that a caring person does not act in the above manner. However, it is important to reiterate that the OSRP staff (including Mrs. H.) define themselves and are predominantly defined by others as truly caring about their students. It should be understood that this contradiction symbolizes and dramatizes sentiments that were expressed in interviews with other students and parents. I will briefly present a sample of these data. First, consider the following parental reactions to the substitute parenting that Brian and Joyce received within the program. These brief interactions are reminiscent of those between Mrs. H., Jen and Jen's mother. Then, listen to Patricia and Joyce (OSRP students) as they express their reactions to Mrs. H.'s caring posture toward them:

Brian's mom: Brian was going to sign up for the army and I think it would have been good for him to go, but he got out of it.

BH: Was he unsure, or what?

BM: The counselor at OSRP talked him out of it.

BH: And how did you feel about that?

BM: Well I sort of wanted him to go [into the army] to mature a little more before college. Cause to me he isn't mature. And he's only a young child anyway. He's only seventeen when he graduates.

. . .

Joyce's mom: I've had to tell her [Mrs. H.] that this is my child and I will make the decision, you know, because that's the way I feel. Mrs. H. tried telling me that Joyce is prejudiced, and she most certainly isn't. That really ticked me off when she said that. She told Joyce that, too, that she was prejudiced. That must put a damper on how she feels about Mrs. H.

. . .

BH: What's she [Mrs. H.] doing wrong?

Patricia: She tells us that we're wrong about things. It's like, "Shut up, man. If I want to do that then I'm gonna do that." You know?

BH: Did you have a problem with her expressing her opinion?

Patricia: She was trying to say my opinion's wrong. But that's my opinion. And that's the way I feel. And she's telling me that I shouldn't feel that way. Shut up, lady. It's just that.

. . .

Joyce: She's [Mrs. H. is] too, I don't know, motherlike. She drives people nuts. And she gets on your case.

BH: Does anybody like the mothering and feel that they need it?

Joyce: Maybe some of them do. But, I mean, the ones that I talk to personally, they don't really like it that well.

Both Brian's mother and Joyce's mother experienced OSRP staff as intrusive. The first complained that OSRP staff had counseled Brian to stay out of the military, when this had been her first choice for her son. Joyce's mom was annoyed at the staff wrongfully labeling Joyce as prejudiced. As students, Patricia and Joyce are like most of their peers in that they resist staff intervention into areas of their lives that they consider to be private. They feel resentful when they are told that they are "wrong about things" or when a staff worker gets on their case. These students take exception to staff who attempt to impose their (largely middle-class) values and norms upon them.

These and other interview data illustrate that young people have definite understandings of the concepts of private and public. Despite (or perhaps because of) staff members' genuine caring about the young people, educators sometimes fail to recognize this public-private distinction. When staff cross over into the private domain, they often do not interpret this in the same way as their students do, that is, as an intrusion into areas that are inappropriate in a teacher-student relationship. Instead, staff see acts like advising, correcting, or representing students' best interests as manifestations of their genuine caring, and would be hurt to learn of the often well hidden negative student reactions.

It seems that the kinds of misunderstandings exemplified here are inevitable, given the staff's low opinion of the students and their parents, their understanding that they are entitled to act as substitute parents, and significant social class differences between staff and students. Within this context, caring is not the positive relationship defined by Noddings (1992) in which people truly listen to one another and try to understand each other's perspectives. Instead, it is a form of objectification. If you comprehend others to be your inferior in a number of ways, it becomes easier to believe in the worst of intentions. If you have a legitimate responsibility to parent others, it is inevitable that your active interest in their well-being will eventually bring you into conflict with their real parent or parents.

The staff's low opinion of the parents has its origin in the program's conservative ideology of hope. These ideas contribute to this process by focusing on the parents as the blameworthy party in the students' at-risk status. If social institutions (including schools) are viewed as "open," it is only reasonable to blame the students and their parents for their at-risk status. The stereotyping of the parents as deficient allows and even encourages the staff to take over parenting as a gesture of good will toward the students. If staff see the parents as being inadequate, then their intervention should make a positive contribution to helping the students improve themselves through better parental guidance.

In conclusion, the staff's negative stereotyping of the parents, their decision to act as substitute parents, and their conflicts with parents are related to social class and ideological factors. The program ideology requires that its adherents must at least surreptitiously seek someone to blame for the students' at-risk status. The staff selectively interpret their communications with parents, identifying them as possessing deficits that are responsible for this set of circumstances. Social class differences between staff and parents enter into this question because the former see a plethora of valid reasons for looking down on the latter. This makes the process of objectification and negative stereotyping easier for them to accomplish.

In the next chapter, I will discuss the relationship between the program, the students, their parents, and the schools. It will be argued that the program does little to set a framework within which the students can voice their opinions about the schools. Again, this is theorized as being related to ideological and social class factors within the program that serve to resist communication.

NOTE

1. Of course, I too am an adult who related to them in a rather short-term way, by entering their lives and then leaving within a limited period of time. Perhaps they shared these thoughts with me because of the different quality of relationship that I had with them. In addition to the normal promises of confidentiality, and so forth, I held no power or authority over them and made every effort to take the time to show genuine and uncritical interest in what they were thinking about and doing in their lives.

6

Mixed Perceptions of the Schools

OSRP students attend various schools within their communities. The vast majority of the River City students attend either River City Senior High School or Highland Senior High School,[1] and most Springfield students attend Springfield Senior High School. Those who do not attend these high schools are either attending one of the middle schools in the community or are registered in a special education or a Catholic school. This chapter will discuss the views that various groups within OSRP have of the schools. The opinions may be interpreted as generic perspectives on the high schools within these communities. Some comments, however, may be related to a specific school, and these will be notated.

First, I will explore the relationship between the schools and the students, as seen through the eyes of the young people and then their parents. I found that both groups have serious critiques of their community schools. Then this chapter will relate the OSRP staff perspective on these schools. They view them in far more benevolent terms than the students or their parents. It is speculated that this may be related to the fact that many of the staff also work as faculty at these schools or work closely with them on a regular basis. As discussed in chapter 5, instead of blaming the schools for problems relating to their students' lack of academic success, many of the staff put the onus on the families. Finally, the chapter links the above findings to the dominant ideology within the program. I argue that the conservative ideology of hope and the related policy of stifling student critique do not contribute to the development of an effective language with which to criticize nonfamily institutions.

STUDENTS' CRITIQUES OF SCHOOLS

This section and the one that follows explore how the students and their parents view the schools that the children attend. The number of expressed positive feelings were more than offset by a tirade that was critical of schools. As such, the emphasis in this chapter is on critique. Although it omits some of the tributes that were paid to schools and their staff, it does not distort the opinions of the subjects. I made critical analysis the focus of this chapter because it was the major theme communicated to me about the community schools. I offered subjects the opportunity to praise as well as critically assess these institutions, and they generally chose the latter.

The students level a wide and devastating array of commentaries on the schools they attend. I will start with two analyses that are common to almost all OSRP students: teachers do not care and teachers do not respect students. The issue of school racism will then be discussed in relation to the River City schools only. Finally, I will briefly summarize some residual evaluations of the schools by the students.

Teachers Do Not Care

OSRP students detect a lack of caring on the part of their teachers. This means that they largely experience their teachers as not connecting emotionally with them and of going through their daily routines in an alienated fashion. Consider the words of a variety of students on this issue:

Latoya: One of my teachers talked to me. He said, "Failing is my game." He say he don't care if we fail because he still gonna get paid. So he teaches summer school!

                                    • • •

Regina: Teachers are there to help us but then half the time they have another teacher come in and they're standing around talking. Then they waste all our time learning.

                                    • • •

BH: How would you change the school if you could?
Patricia: I would have teachers that cared about their students, cared if they passed. And, you know, made them understand easier, and taught them different ways, different methods of teaching, you know? And care about their students. Cause the teacher that don't care, you know, shoot em out in the garbage. . . . Teachers don't care. They can't care, you know. Like they'll teach you something, but, if say you don't understand it and you go ask them for help or something, they don't have time for you because they're doing something else.

                                    • • •

BH: So what's the barrier between the school as it presently is and yourself? Why don't you do better in school and enjoy it more?
Early: Why I don't do better? It's the teachers: if they don't care, why should you [students] care?

OSRP students are annoyed at having to endure uncaring teachers. Latoya even suggests that teachers have a vested interest in failing students so that they can earn money teaching summer school. Students conclude that the teachers do not care from a variety of observations about their behavior: they socialize with other teachers during instructional time, they do not work hard enough to find ways to reach all the students in the class, and they do not have (or take?) the time to help individual students with their academic problems. According to Early, this attitude affects students like himself because he sees the malaise spreading from the teachers to their students, "If they don't care, why should you care?"

Teachers Do Not Respect Students

Students related a plethora of stories with this single theme: teachers do not respect us. From these students' point of view, teachers do not listen to them, they take out their personal frustrations on them and treat them as if they are less than human. Consider a small sampling of stories I was told with this focus:

Lamont: This is because there was papers I was passin' out and he said I didn't have permission to pass them out. I said that I made a mistake and I tryin' to talk to him. I just told him to leave me alone.

BH: You tried to explain to this teacher that it was just an honest mistake?

Lamont: He told me not to talk because he wasn't talkin' to me. And I just said forget it. Leave me alone.

BH: What should I understand from this little story you just told me?

Lamont: If I'm trying to explain somethin' to somebody and he don't hear it, I'm goin' to get an attitude.

BH: So you spoke but you weren't listened to?

Lamont: Ya. I was told. I wasn't listened to. So I got an attitude.

BH: Does that show you lack of respect?

Lamont: Ya. Not my lack of respect, but the other [the teacher's].

. . .

BH: You think that school officials and teachers have hurt you or do you think that they have helped you?

Obuagu: I think both.

BH: Can you talk to me about that?

Obuagu: Well when they hurt you, you learn from your hurts and your mistakes and stuff like that. And things they teach you you learn too. And that's what you need to succeed in life . . .

BH: And how do they hurt you?

Obuagu: Probably words and remarks that they say.

BH: The kind of words and remarks that are hurtful to people?

Obuagu: Uh huh.

BH: What effect do hurtful words from a teacher have on a person?

Obuagu: Make them start thinkin' at it. Maybe they should drop out of school. Maybe it's true what they say.

. . .

Felicia: We had to put our locks on our lockers just the first day of school. We put our locks on our lockers. And a lot of kids would surround around the halls and he [my teacher] was talking to a[nother] teacher and we was, we just went and looked downstair, cause we sit down and there was a balcony on our stairs, and we looked down a balcony. He started yellin' at us and said, "Come here," and asked us about our lockers and everything. And then he had said, "Now you tell me that you're sorry and that you will not go down those stairs no more." My cousin said it but I said I don't have to say that. And he just made me mad on that day. Cause he was tryin' to force me to say that. And

I'm not gonna let him force me to do something I don't want to do.

BH: And you didn't have the feeling that you did anything wrong, is that what it boils down to?

Felicia: Most likely, ya. Just because we looked over the stair don't mean he gotta make a big deal about it. He could a said, "Could you guys come over here?" Well he just had to make a big deal about it.

BH: Are you saying then that he didn't treat you with the amount of respect that you considered to be reasonable?

Felicia: He didn't. He didn't respect what I wanted. He didn't respect me at all, put it that way. All we did was look at the stair. He could have just said, "Could you come over here? You're not supposed to do that."

Lamont, Obuagu, and Felicia agree with each other that teachers sometimes abuse their authority by using hurtful words that show a lack of respect for students. Lamont indicates that this incident has taught him that it is the teacher who tells and it is the student's role to listen. But he also concludes that this rule shows a basic lack of respect for students. The teacher is perceived as attacking his self-respect. He notes that this kind of treatment led *him* to "get an attitude." Obuagu comments that some students might react to these kinds of treatments by thinking about dropping out. Felicia's response is to save her dignity by simply refusing to apologize for something that she does not feel merits it.

The above observations focus on what OSRP students see as teachers' lack of respect. The students feel relatively powerless within the school structure to constructively react to these types of situations. Josh's comments go right to the heart of this feeling of powerlessness:

BH: Say you went to the principal, what's the principal likely to say?

Josh: He'd probably say, "Well, that's the way it is," or something stupid like that.

BH: Just back him [the teacher] up?

Josh: Ya.

BH: Do you ever think he would take sides against the teacher?

Josh: Probably not. So that's how principals and assistant principals are. They believe the teacher over you, and that's stupid. When the teachers write you up, they can just put anything on there and if you didn't even do that then you get busted for it.

Josh does not just reveal feelings of powerlessness. He also uncovers an understanding by students that they are sometimes the victims of arbitrary authorities who are not above lying or deception. This is a harsh criticism of schools and their staff. But it is not unique to this student. For example, Dewitt complains that some teachers are like this one who "had the nerve to grab me and yank me. . . . Cause some teachers, they'll try to take advantage of you and you have to put your foot down and tell em, 'Look, I'm not no doggie. Better treat me like I'm a person.'"

LaKesia comments on being made to feel "dumb" by her social studies teacher: "My social studies teacher, because she's the type of teacher that thinks if you don't get that question, you're dumb. If you don't get the right answer, you're dumb. If you don't know it, you're dumb. I don't like that. . . . She make me feel like I can't learn in there, and that I'll never pass in there." Her next comment refers to the arbitrary ways in which her English teacher feels she can treat the whole class: "Sometimes my English teacher, she get mad and just take it out on everybody. She just start yellin' if you ask her a question. She won't pay you no attention. . . . Cause like if I need her help on somethin', she won't pay me no attention. It's like I'm not even there."

Wateef sees a basic inequality in power between teachers and students: "Just because teachers have power to punish you without reason gives them no right to disrespect you. Respect is earned, not given. If you're [as] mean to a teacher as they are to you, they can expel you from school."

I do not present these criticisms of teachers as a blanket denunciation of the latter group. Nor do I intend to argue their validity or invalidity. They are presented simply as evidence that the Springfield and River City OSRP students perceive their teachers as being disrespectful toward them in a variety of ways, for different reasons, and with a mixture of results. Later in this chapter, I will juxtapose these student perceptions with those held by OSRP staff.

Racism

Racism within schools is only perceived to be an issue by the River City students. This issue resonates strongly with them, at the same time that it seems irrelevant to the Springfield students in their all-white suburb. The predominantly African American River City students told me that they perceive racism within their schools as originating from three different sources: teachers, fellow students, and the school itself. I will present some of their comments in these three areas.

Teacher Racism.
BH: Have you ever seen or heard of teachers being racist?
LaKesia: Yes. A teacher I had last year is a math teacher and he's good to call [someone] a nigger to their face. He don't care. He was about to call me one. I was like, "Call me one." I was like, I don't care where I'm at. I was like I don't. I was like, "That's not right. You don't call me a nigger." He wouldn't want me to talk about his race so I was like, "Tell me. Say it right now." I don't care who he is. I would have fought him. I don't care, cause he had no right to call me a nigger.

· · ·

BH: What happened to you?
Student One[2]: I failed the second grade cause my teacher didn't like black people. I think that's dumb on their part. If they don't like black people, just pass them on, you know?
Student Two: I know. If I was in that situation, if I didn't like somebody, I was a teacher, I'd pass them on. Just like that. And get them out of my way.

Student Racism.
BH: So how do you feel about the school as a whole? Are you glad to go there?
Andy: Ya, it's an okay school but sometimes there's like racial things. Like blacks versus whites. A lot of times, after school they fight or they get jumped or something.
BH: And does this make you feel like you're gonna be next?

Andy: I just like try to watch myself and stuff like that.

BH: So you try to stay out of blacks' way?

Andy: Ya. I know a lot of black people, they're nice. But some of them, I don't know, they're just like mean. They were brought up that way or something. I don't know.

BH: Are there whites that you also try to keep your distance from?

Andy: No.

BH: Do you feel that the school has a definite racial tension between blacks and whites?

Andy: Ya.

BH: Do you think something could be done about it?

Andy: No.

BH: Why?

Andy: I don't know. It's the way people are. I don't think they're going to change their minds. Nobody's gonna tell them what to do.

(Andy is one of two whites in the River City OSRP group)

· · ·

BH: What about race. Is that an issue in the school?

LaKesia: Yes. Some people don't like black people. It'd bother me, you know, if they called me a nigger or something. But usually they say nothin'. Like sometimes when I passed like to throw something in the garbage and that person just about come past and they get an attitude and start yelling that I can't stand you people. That really make me mad. It make me want to fight. And I'll do it.

School Racism.

BH: How would you change that school if you could change it?

Obuagu: I get more black staffs. That school need a lot of changes. There's too many to name.

BH: Can you tell me why you think it's important to have more black teachers?

Obuagu: So when a black student come to the school, he will feel that he fit in, he fit in like that.

BH: Do you have any black teachers right now?

Obuagu: Mr. Stevenson. But he's not really a teacher. He's the in-school restriction teacher.

BH: So how does that make you feel about the place?

Obuagu: When you first start off at the school, you feel uncomfortable. You been there about two or three years, you cope with it. You just there to get your education and get out.

The River City students view some of their peers and teachers as being racist. African American and white students and teachers seem guarded around each other, alert to the potential for racism to surface. This takes place within schools that are also viewed as being racist by the African American youth. Obuagu is wary of the hiring practices. Another student is suspicious of "their" promotion practices. LaKesia thinks that the school permits racism to continue:

LaKesia: They really don't pay no attention. Say like if I get in a fight and I fight because she called me a nigger. They won't believe it. They don't want to believe it.

BH: Are there things done in that school to try to encourage good feeling between the races

there, or is just nothing done?
LaKesia: Nothing done. Just nothing. Just do what you have to do.

There is a certain level of acceptance by the students that this racism is inevitable:

BH: Would you say that the teachers are aware of this [racism]?
Quionna: The teachers are aware of it. But if they try to say something to either a black student or a white student, the student will probably get mad and say, "Well you must like the black people." You know, something like that. And if she's talking to a black person, she'd say, "Well, you must like the white people." And I don't think that's right.

I have attempted to explicate some of the racial tensions and emotions that are inherent to the two high schools in River City. Blacks and whites and students and teachers all experience racial tension as part of their everyday existence in those school buildings. There is an "us" versus "them" mentality on the part of many of the students, all of whom can quickly tell a story about racial incidents in and around the schools. At the same time, there is acceptance that this is simply part of the reality of high school life. One is aware of it, and yet it is officially ignored. It is morally wrong, and yet the schools appear to be powerless to correct it.

This section has attempted to give the reader a view of some of the critiques that OSRP students carry around with them in relation to their schools. I have presented their perceptions of their teachers' "I don't care" attitudes and their lack of respect for students. In addition, River City students' views of racism within the schools have been shown. Grave as these evaluations are, they represent only a small portion of the critiques made of the schools. I paraphrase some of their additional concerns below:

The change from elementary scheduling (where there is only one teacher for all or most core subjects) to middle and high school scheduling (where students have a multitude of teachers for roughly forty minutes each) ruins the close and caring relationship with my teachers that I need in order to succeed. (Lamont, Obuagu)

The curriculum is boring, irrelevant, and dominated by teacher talk and meaningless pen and paper exercises, copying, and so forth. (Andy, Brian, Davette, Felicia, LaKesia, Latoya, Louis, Nick, Obuagu, Patricia, Regina, Shalimar, Terry, Yolanda)

I react poorly to a place where it is implied or suggested that I am dumb. (Argina, Joyce, LaKesia, Patricia, Raquel)

Suspension is an illogical and stupid form of punishment. (Early, Lamont)

The best part of coming to school is socializing with my friends. (Brian, Dewitt, Hakim, Jen, Kente, Latoya, Nick, Patricia, Raquel, Terry)

Teachers focus on the fast pace of their curriculum, ignoring the range of abilities and needs of their students. (Terry)

Teachers do not teach to ensure that all students learn. Too many students drop out or are pushed out. (Latoya, Patricia, Yolanda)

Schools have far too many rules that depersonalize students, for example, punishing all for one person's wrongdoing. (Josh, Judith, Latoya, Louis, Nick)

School is an unnecessary evil that bears no relationship to real work out there. I endure it just because I need it to get a job, or I endure it because my mom will kick me out of the house if I don't. (Nick, Josh, Louis, Regina)

These students' views are insightful, critical, and emotionally felt. They are insightful because, as a group, they represent a wisdom that I know they did not read about in the education literature. And yet they are critical of many of the same practices that scholars of education extensively research and rediscover by observing and questioning within schools (e.g., see Cusick, 1973; Goodlad, 1984; Powell et al., 1985; Sizer, 1984; and Wehlage et al., 1989, as reviewed in chapter 1). Finally, one senses an emotional reaction to these environments in the words that students choose to describe events and practices. Their stories are not abstractions or academic exercises to them: they involve real people whom they interact with daily, often in ways that are not pleasing to them.

PARENTS' CRITIQUES OF SCHOOLS

The Springfield and River City parents generally agree with each other that the schools are not doing a good job in meeting the needs of their children. In the words of one parent, their kids are "falling in the cracks." The River City parents have two additional apprehensions. One is what they perceive as a problem of control in River City Senior High School. The other is a more pervasive feeling that the schools are racist in their approach to teaching their children. These are seen as having significant and negative consequences for their children.

Kids are Falling In the Cracks

OSRP parents say that their children are not receiving an acceptable education in their schools. Furthermore, they feel that school personnel are permitting this situation to continue unabated. They see a lack of caring for individual students and a relaxed attitude on the part of teachers and principals toward their own job performance:

Andy's mom: I think that Andy's doing okay there because he's got a good head on his shoulders. I think that another student who didn't have the same, maybe, attitude as him might kind of fall in the cracks in that system.

. . .

Obuagu's mom: In my opinion, Obuagu's just a student. I mean, Obuagu is, it's hard to say. Everyone is lumped in a group. You can't do that. He's generalized with everybody else. He's lost in the shuffle. Unless he does something really outstanding, they're not gonna really take any notice of him. And in my opinion, he's very talented. And if he gets the right push, he could really go far. . . . He can't really get the help he needs at school.

. . .

Regina's mom: At the school, you just sit at a desk, you know, and the teacher's probably picking his nose. I don't know. It's hard for the kids to get help up there because there's so many kids crammed in one classroom, you know? And the teacher doesn't have time for anybody else, you know? . . . They sit around. I've been in that school walking around. And them teachers are sitting at their desk drinking a bottle of pop or drinking their coffee or something. And you know, the kids are just shooting the breeze.

. . .

Josh's mom: I don't think they care. They just want their money, you know. They get their daily allotment for each kid, and I think that's all they want is money. . . . A kid misses school, they're not interested in why he missed it, or you know, if he has a problem. They just want him there.

. . .

Nancy's mom: When Nancy went to junior high, they found this attitude problem. They notified me. I went in for meetings, team meetings, everything. It seems like the senior high kinda just like lets them go. I don't know if it's me or if it's cause how I feel, but she's just lost in the shuffle. As long as they're doing their work in that class, the teacher don't care about the attitude.

These parents are united in one clear message: there are too many students in the school and in the classes for anybody to care about them as individuals. The result is that their children become generalized as part of an anonymous crowd, despite their distinctiveness. A few are important, but the majority are destined to remain nameless. The parents see teachers responding to this large, anonymous context in two related ways: by saying "I don't care" and "I'm in it for the money." High school teachers "don't care about the attitude . . . sit around . . . pick their noses." They do not push their students to achieve to the limits of their abilities. When the secretary phones a parent concerning an absence, they are taking part in an anonymous process. The perception is that the secretary does not know or care about why the child is absent. The secretary is a representation of what the parent is feeling about the school as a whole: anonymity, money, numbers, lack of caring. As the parents see it, this environment of malaise allows their children to simply fall in the cracks.

There are two remaining parental critiques to consider, both of which focus on River City.

River City Senior High School: A Problem of Control

It is important to understand that River City has two high schools: an older urban high school that has traditionally served the black and the poor (River City High School, or "High School"), and a newer suburban school (Highland) that is predominantly white and more middle class in its student population. The parents of Highland students have few complaints about the general demeanor of the school, but the parents of High School attenders express very negative views. They read in the paper and hear talk about the fights, drug busts, and other disturbances that routinely occur at High School. They perceive the school to be out of control:

LaKesia's mom: You know, they respected Dr. Marks [a former principal]. They say he was mean and he did this and he did that. But they respected him.
BH: So you'd like to see maybe a little bit more discipline in that school?
LM: Yes.

. . .

Lamont's mom: I think the whole school should be shut down, you know. Cause he's [Lamont is] not the only child that came out of there with a problem with the school and all that.
BH: What do you see as being the problem with the school?
LM: I think they should get like a real principal there who can really guide the kids and somebody that the kids will really listen to. And go with him, you know? I mean her or whoever. The two last principals they had up there really wasn't, they didn't really need to be there.
BH: So are you saying that you believe the principal should be stricter than she is?
LM: I think she should. Ya.

. . .

Latoya's mom: I don't like the school myself. It's just like it's a rough school.
BH: Is there something that the staff could be doing to kind of settle the place down?
LM: Try to get better control over the students.
BH: How could they do that?
LM: I don't know.
BH: Where do you feel that there's a lack of control?
LM: There's always some kind of fights and stuff like that. And I feel they could have better control of that some kind of way. . . . I wanted her [Latoya] to go to Highland.
BH: I see. And somehow you think that's a better school?
LM: Yes I do.

The parents' call for stricter control is a reaction to their perception of a lack of supervision at High School. They hold the principal personally responsible for setting the tone of the school as a whole. As such, she is compared unfavorably with the "respected Dr. Marks," or "somebody that the kids will really listen to."

River City High Schools Are Racist

When parents express themselves about racism and racist incidents within River City schools, they are addressing a variety of issues. Like their children, they observe student, staff, and institutional racism in the schools. In addition to understanding the effects of racism on themselves and their children, they develop ideas as to why the situation has evolved in this way, deal with the problems as they emerge, and propose solutions to the problem of racism. I will present parental responses in all these areas. In doing so, I will focus on the voices of two African American moms because they were especially articulate in expressing their thoughts on this topic. My purpose is to clarify parental visions and concerns in this sensitive and emotional area. Let us start by considering the problem of racism in interactions among students, as seen from the perspective of Regina's mother (Regina is the only white female at the River City site):

BH: Are there tensions between black and white students in Regina's school?

RM: Ya. A lot.

BH: Does that affect Regina?

RM: In a way. She walked down the hall the first week of school and she had her book bag on her shoulder. And she walked by a group of kids, and one happened to be a colored girl. And I guess the book bag brushed up against her. And she turned around and she goes, "Move me. If you bump into me again I'm gonna beat your face in." You know. And it's not a good atmosphere for kids to learn in.

Yolanda's mom is typical of the African American parents who detect racism among white students as well as white teachers in River City schools:

YM: Well, I have to say this. There is racism that exists in the school, and I don't like that.

BH: What form does the racism take? Is it on the part of the staff or the students?

YM: It's the staff. Yes, definitely staff. Also some students. They were writing things like "KKK" on the lockers, and "niggers" this, and, you know, things like that.

BH: How do you think that affects a young person like Yolanda?

YM: It makes them angry, they become angry. We sit down and talk about it. I guess for me as a parent, it hurts more than I get angry. It hurts me that my child has to deal with the reality that it exists. You know, because as a parent, you always want to shield your child from any unpleasant experience. I wouldn't wish that none of my children would have to face what the reality of it is. You face it from the beginning, you know. And just for her to have to face it, it hurted me. She was angry.

Her immediate solution to racial incidents is to "sit down and talk" with Yolanda:

Me and her sit down and we talk. Yolanda and me are friends first. I'm her mother, yes. But I'm her friend. Okay? And she will tell me little incidents where there would be, she would say, "This teacher's prejudice," and stuff like that. Which gives me the opportunity to be able to talk about the experiences that I have had. You know what I tell her? There's a bad bunch in every group. Just like some black people. I say, "You see how some black people, they ignorant and they say racist things to white people and stuff like that? It's the same with white people. All white aren't bad." I don't want my child to grow up thinking all white people think the same or all white people are the same.

Yolanda's mom perceives that racism is something more than a matter of some students or some staff members being racist. She is concerned about the school's response to these kinds of behaviors, and proposes her own solution to the problem.

BH: Is the administration doing its job properly toward a young person like Yolanda?

YM: To be honest, I don't think so. Because of the fact that racism exists, okay? And if we accept it, the reality of it. We have to say, "Okay, let's deal with this problem. Does it exist? Yes? No?" We say it, but what do we do about it?

BH: So you don't see the school really attacking this problem?

YM: No, I don't see the school being actively involved in trying to solve the problem. . . . I feel as though if we dealt with the fact that it does exist as a reality, that this racism is there, and let's come together black, white, Hispanic, whatever nationality you may be. Let's come together as young adults and let's talk about what things we can do to bridge this gap. And I think that's where the administration also should be looking at as well as, you know, talking to the students. You know, get the students' opinions about things. I don't think they involve the students enough in the issues that's going on in the world today. I think that's a big mistake.

Early's mom, on the other hand, interprets the problem differently. From her perspective, economic, educational, and social disparities are serious problems affecting the black community. She sees the schools as institutions that reinforce African American dependence upon whites:

It seems to me like these young black kids is just going right down the drain. . . . They are not getting no teaching in the schools. I think like black people as a race just goin down to destruction or something. . . . I don't see the schools are meeting the black kids' needs because if they did, black people would not be in this condition that they are today. And with all this, there's unemployment, and you can't get jobs and factories are moving out. Can't get no jobs for kids. I think something really gonna happen very bad. I think if it is going to be a change, I think something gonna happen. It gonna be quite a riot. Something I think gonna happen very bad. Some of the people can't get jobs. They don't care no more, you know. They just don't care. . . . I don't think any of the white man's schools meet the black kids' needs. . . . Because they are not teaching them, they are not teaching them that when they grow up they should do things for themselves. They teach them that they should go to white people and ask white people for jobs. And I think that they're not teaching them the true knowledge about themself. . . . I think that black people was put in slavery and black people will have to take themselves out. And I don't think the white man gonna teach black kids to rise above them. I think if you teach them, you got to teach them to keep them below him.

Her solution to this problem is separate schools for black children: "Whoever teaches your kids controls your future. And if we had the proper schooling, we would be equal with him. We wouldn't have to go to him for everything. . . . All the schools is controlled by whites. If the kid's having problems in school, you go to the school and they talk to you. And they don't do anything to help the kids. . . . I think the solution is for black people to unite and get their own schools for their children."

These three parents agree that racism exists as a serious problem within River City schools. It is a problem among students, between students and staff, as well as an inherent part of the institutions themselves. For the two African American moms, racism is seen as having social and economic consequences for their community, ranging from emotional hurts to economic vulnerability. Two distinctly different solutions include schools' promoting integration policies and separate African

American schools.

In summary, the parents (like the students) have a list of grievances with the schools in their communities. There is a general feeling that the schools allow kids to fall in the cracks. Parents sense a lack of caring on the part of schools toward children who are not exceptional. Within River City, the poor, urban school traditionally attended by most African American youth is perceived as being out of control. African American parents feel a presence of racism within and around the schools, with social and economic consequences for their children.

We have seen that students and their parents have serious critiques of the schools in their communities. In the next chapter, these critiques will be placed within a context of educational literature that attempts to explain their relationship to social factors such as class and race. For now, it is important to understand that these critiques are intensely felt and related to negative experiences that are endured by many. I will now present OSRP staff's perceptions of these same schools. They represent a strikingly different perspective of how well the schools are meeting the needs of their students.

THE SCHOOLS AS BENIGN

When OSRP staff look at their students' schools, they do not see the same places that have just been described by students and their parents. This different outlook is no doubt linked to the fact that these two groups come from different worlds, have different roles within these institutions, and have different interests in relation to them. To a large extent, the staff view the schools as being well-intentioned, although imperfect, institutions. Consider some of their descriptions of how schools impact upon at-risk students:

Gerald: I was teaching in the inner city part-time and I saw a teacher physically assault students. I mean physically assault students. . . . I can't believe this is going on. I mean I saw a teacher smack a child in the face in front of everybody. This child was a fifth grader. I said, "What the hell.". . . And [I thought] maybe, just maybe the parent probably said, "Do whatever you want to him." I've seen that before. . . . There are many schools here in this county that have no minority hiring. So a child of color can go from kindergarten to grade twelve without seeing any minority role models at all. That's an issue. . . . There are many, many kids who are coming in being diagnosed and misdiagnosed as learning disabled. And the misdiagnosis is even more prevalent because in the minds unfortunately of many educators, kids are very disposable. You get them in, you get them out. And what that does of course is perpetuate the feeling of failure.

. . .

Louise: There's very little success rate in terms of programming and scheduling policies. Whether it's the attendance policy or if we should recommend maybe a modified day, or maybe particular teachers, or change from one class to another. Those things are generally not possible. Like maybe a particular student would be better off if they had a study hall last period and being permitted to leave. Or a half-day schedule could be arranged for a student to take the four major subjects and then leave the school building.
BH: You can't arrange for that kind of programming as things stand?

Louise: At this time it is impossible.

. . .

Sally: The school can't respond to the needs when you've got budget cuts and that. We
were running a building with sixteen hundred kids without an assistant principal. I mean,
that's ludicrous. There's just a lot of problems with the system: it could be River City, it
could be Springfield, it could be anywhere. You know, it's hard times right now . . . and
education isn't up there on the list anywhere. And we're getting cuts, and it filters down,
you know. And jobs get cut, the numbers in the classes get bigger, all the extras like
gifted and talented. And then it affects morale. And once it affects morale, you got a
teacher who's maybe feeling a little frustrated with, you know, trying to reach kids and
maybe frustrated with themselves. And you can't necessarily take the time out to sit down
with Jenny Jones who's in the background on her own, feeling upset.

These OSRP staff are saying that schools fail to respond to the needs of their
students. They perceive that students who are different from the norm are less likely
to have their concerns addressed by the school system. African American youngsters
are denied the role model of teachers of their own race. Those who do not learn at the
same pace as others are often "misdiagnosed as learning disabled." Students who
might benefit from schedule flexibility find that this is not possible. Teachers who are
getting larger classes and fewer support services suffer from morale problems. As
Gerald, Louise, and Sally see the schools, they are falling short of offering the kinds
of programs that can meet the needs of the at-risk population represented by OSRP.
Yet, these criticisms fall well short of the condemnations expressed by the students
and their parents. They are reasoned and restrained criticisms of an imperfect system.
For example, Gerald's observation of physical assault is tempered by his own
suggestion that a parent may have given the teacher permission to strike the child.
These staff, then, view the schools as imperfect institutions. It seems that their close
ties with them (Louise and Sally are school staff, Gerald is a former employee) do not
encourage or permit these critiques to develop into condemnation.

The remaining OSRP staff are not prepared to criticize schools even as moderately
as Gerald, Louise, and Sally. Instead, they view them in largely benign terms that
sometimes seems to include self-congratulations:

Kevin: The school system offers consistency, stability, boundaries, security. As opposed to
their home lives that are unpredictable, full of cataclysms, unstructured.
BH: Can a school that is predominantly run by white administrators and white teachers
reach out and really meet the needs of black students?
Kevin: Absolutely. [At my school] we've got a committed staff who are empathetic,
altruistic, with uncompromised humanitarian spirit.

. . .

BH: Have the schools failed these kids, as far as you can see?
Jane: Not one bit. Not one bit. I don't think the school or the teachers in the classroom
owe them any more than what they have been giving them. I think it's the students. If
you saw Andy Rooney on "60 Minutes," he said it right. He says the parents and students
(and I use the word loosely) are stupid. Because it's there for the taking and they're so

dumb. He used the word "dumb." They're dumb. They're too dumb to take what's being given to them. The parents are too dumb to take TV away from their kids. They're too dumb to make their kids go to school. The parents are just too dumb to take advantage of what is there for them. And in essence, every teacher over in that school, all seventy of them are saying the same thing, "The parents are just too dumb to make it happen for their kids."

. . .

Tim: I think the school reaches out fairly well to all kids and to these kids at risk. . . . I think we do a pretty good job. And I think because of the OSR Program it helps us to do a good job. . . . We have a lot of different programs here in Springfield, I think that are pretty effective. But do you meet all kids' needs? No, they still don't meet all the kids' needs.

These staff members have a generally positive orientation toward schools and their staff. They are seen as offering "consistency, . . . empathy" (Kevin) and programs (Tim) that are given by the staff to willing and unwilling students (Jane). But this orientation to school has a problem: if these institutions are benign, how can students' lack of success therein be explained? Instead of blaming at least some of the failure on school budgets, programs, and policies (as do the first group of staff), these staff members blame the parents and students for their own failures. They are "too dumb," or not "consistent or stable" enough. There are elements of uncritical self-satisfaction among this group of OSRP staff. Things could perhaps be improved, but most of the blame for any failure within these institutions falls squarely on the shoulders of the parents and children who find themselves at risk.

The staff as a whole talk about different things than the parents or the students when they comment on the effectiveness of schools. The latter speak of emotional experiences that have happened to them and those they know. They speak of hurts, inequities, racism, and unfair situations in personal ways. To the OSRP staff, however, schools have successes and failures in providing services to young people. Failures are described in terms of programming rather than as personal experiences. Schools are viewed as either imperfect or benevolent institutions, making their present organization seem more or less inevitable. What critiques there are seem intellectualized and abstract when compared to the feelings expressed by the parents and students. If there are problems at all, they are somebody else's problems (e.g., those of "dumb" parents). The staff do not focus on many of the concerns of the students and their parents. For example, their analyses do not include staff, institutional, or student racism, uncaring and disrespectful teachers and administrators, a boring, irrelevant curriculum, the "pushing" of students out of schools, or the depersonalization of rules. Instead, there is talk of "programs," "staffing," "scheduling," and "morale." The staff and OSRP families seem miles apart from each other.

This may be related to different experience bases and to the roles through which they interpret the schools. These distinct perspectives on the schools seem somehow inherent in the personal history one has had within such institutions. The staff members share experiences of personal accomplishment and achievement within schools: they are all academic success stories who have graduated from undergraduate and/or graduate programs. At-risk students, however, have shared their histories of failure and frustration within schools with me (many of which have been included in this chapter). It is likely that their parents share similar personal histories within schools (Alexander et al., 1978). Thus, dissimilar experiences within schools may at least partly explain their different reactions to these institutions.

In addition, role differences may play a part in this process. Most OSRP staff work in the schools attended by their students; those who are not so employed interact regularly with school staff as part of carrying out their OSRP staff role. Lortie found that most teachers tend to be individualistic, conservative, and conventional (1975). He postulated that this is related to recruitment factors into the profession and to the experience of teaching under current organizational arrangements. Additionally, earning one's living and gaining one's career identity from schools as a professional staff member are likely related to the staff's reluctance to seriously critique schools. Students and parents, on the other hand, have a different perspective of schools because they carry out different roles in relation to them. They experience high schools in the temporary roles of student and parent of student. Their interest is narrower in the sense that they tend to approach the institution trying to realize their own interests. When these are threatened by academic weakness, their reactions to the institutions tend to be personal because they confront staff who they believe to be responsible for particular problems. Their accusations tend to be emotional because they have a significant personal stake in the outcomes of the services that the school provides.

CONCLUSION

The students' and their parents' comments offer a number of serious critiques of schools. Yet, with the exception of African Americans' racial identity, there is no mention of any collective identity or understanding of cooperative interests among others like themselves. Analysis rarely goes beyond the quest for individualistic upward mobility. The one notable exception is Early's mother, who discussed the need for separate, African American schools where young people could learn to be independent of the white man. This is an important statement of collective identity based on race. But, on the whole, the parents and students do not use a language of critique that may be reasonably understood as being race based or class based. Despite OSRP's guideline that one must fall below the poverty line to obtain entrance, class identification is very tenuous for these students and their parents. This is evidenced by the fact that when I asked students about their social class of origin, almost all identified themselves as being middle class. In addition, most were not familiar with an approximation of the term's conventional meaning, with about half misinterpreting my question as a reference to one of their high school courses (i.e., their social *studies* class). OSRP students simply do not use language that suggests any basic comprehension on their part that they are living in a class society.

This degree of naiveté on the part of the students is not surprising, given OSRP's informal curriculum. Chapter 4 discussed the extent to which staff seek to control the expression of what they refer to as negative critiques of institutions by students. It was reported that the program offers no opportunity for students and their parents to voice class-based or racially based critiques because these are thought of by the staff as being negative. OSRP staff express their ideological support for existing social institutions like schools and the economic system, despite obvious problems that their students are having in relation to these. As such, the program itself may be seen as attempting to stifle any latent class-based and racially based societal critiques, replacing them with the conservative ideology of hope.

It is important to reemphasize that the program's main goal is to integrate these young people within schools so that they increase their performance there. Yet, the program does not address (or allow the students to address) any of the concerns that they and their parents have expressed above. Instead, the staff rest within the safe boundaries of the conservative ideology of hope. Given the failure of OSRP to make headway on its central goal of integrating at-risk students into their schools (chapter 2), it seems clear that institutional critiques like the ones raised above by the students and their parents will not easily be replaced with this ideology. Experiences of perceived injustice are hard to explain within a conservative ideology that promises upward mobility. The program might be successful in encouraging students and their parents to mouth its official ideology, but this does not supplant their experiences within social institutions like schools and the economy. Hence, the staff and students/parents talk past each other, communicating their different experiences. This is predictably associated with deadlock and an inability to achieve program goals.

NOTES

1. River City Senior High School is informally referred to as "High School" within the community. Highland is referred to by its name. Perhaps this reflects the fact that for years, the former was the only high school in the community.

2. I cannot identify these speakers by name because this interview was transcribed from an audio recording of a group of students.

7

Another Lost Opportunity

Chapter 1 reviewed the current literature exploring the relationship between at-risk students and their schools. I argued that there are external forces acting upon schools, as well as internal organizational factors that help to explain how at-risk student status is created and maintained. Many of the observations of researchers were found in the relationships between OSRP students and their schools. For example, students' and parents' complaints relating to a lack of caring within schools are consistent with findings made separately by Cusick (1973), Powell et al. (1985), and Sizer (1984). As well, the racism and racial tensions within schools as reported by Wright (1987) and Solomon (1989) found themselves well represented in the experiences of OSRP's River City members.

There are two areas in which most OSRP staff, students, and parents differ significantly from the literature on at-risk students: that is, in their naiveté about tracking and social class barriers to upward mobility. Whenever tracking was mentioned (I asked all the students and staff how they felt about tracks and track placements), it was met with innocuous acceptance. None of the research observations reported above concerning the relationship between track placement and life chances were observed by or personally experienced by OSRP members. Tracking seems unproblematic and unimportant; they do not perceive the students' lower track status as a barrier to any future success.

The second barrier to upward mobility is social class. In contrast to the research literature, these young people do not perceive their life chances as being limited by the tenuous economic position of their parents. They are unable to express knowledge of a relationship between social class and life chances, but sense the importance of class around them. For example, the River City students often told me that Highland is the "better" high school. Those in Springfield know that "preps" are snobs who think they are better than others. OSRP students generally experience school as an alien place (except for socializing with their peers). Yet, they have no explanation for these feelings and observations. They have a limited frame in which to fit their rather negative personal experiences. How is it that these young people see certain aspects of their high schools as being clearly deficient, while they are accepting of others as mere details of life? Why do they not anticipate that class, race, gender, or track placement will have an impact upon their prospects for achieving career aspirations in the future? Is this not surprising in light of the fact that they exhibit great insight and sensitivity in many of their other observations about how the system works?

The most plausible explanation is that their society provides them with an ideology that places certain defined limits on their vision. I have referred to the prevailing ideology as the "conservative ideology of hope." It addresses itself to a politically sensitive area: that is, the origin and maintenance of inequality within a society that characterizes itself as a democracy. Prevailing inequalities are explained by these ideas, and have the effect of legitimating them. Hence, inequalities become just another element of context, another given in social life to be accepted or worked around. The students' naiveté on these issues is an important finding of this study. It suggests that OSRP is successful in reinforcing a tacit acceptance of the status quo, despite its failure to meet its stated objectives in terms of school integration.

Why do OSRP staff maintain an individualistic orientation that favors hope over the recognition of societal barriers? First, it should be noted that this tendency has been found in other contexts (e.g., McLeod, 1987; McLaren, 1986). McLeod found that the teachers in his urban setting reinforce the individual achievement ideology as a strategy to deal with the constant threat of student misbehavior. It is likely that OSRP staff adopt the program ideology for this reason as well. However, the overriding explanation is that personal experience and U.S. culture provide staff with this influential set of ideas. It has often been observed that U.S. culture promulgates a belief in individual achievement. For example, Ryan (1971) argues that Americans overwhelmingly believe in the appealing notion of the United States as a land of opportunity. Americans think that everyone starts out with the same opportunities, with some using them and others not. He calls this a belief in fair play, where individuals who display ability and directed effort are thought to deserve greater resources from an essentially fair system of social stratification. From this perspective, OSRP staff have simply internalized their culture's dominant ideological position.

This (like any ideology) simplifies vision. The implicit view of society held by program staff is that it is acceptably organized and/or it cannot be changed. Thus, failure is seen as primarily individual in nature, to be blamed on inadequate socialization by parents. It is interesting that other socialization agents (e.g., the school, youth groups, the church, OSRP) are not similarly singled out for condemnation. Perhaps this is because these are identified as being part of the broader societal context and are beyond critique because of their sponsorship by elite groups. The singular and one-sided focus on the family, however, seems undeserved, especially in light of the contradictory evidence concerning the nature of the relationships between students and their parents.

The picture that emerges from this study is that of one socialization institution (OSRP) blaming another (families) for improper execution of their responsibilities. This implies that the schools and the state act as if they are the most effective socialization agents for these young people. No doubt there is some logic to this accusation: material and social conditions of poverty have been found elsewhere to be related to the establishment of circumstances making it less likely that students will be socialized for school success (Bernstein, 1977; Bloom, Davis, and Hess, 1965; Bourdieu, 1977; Bowles and Gintis, 1976; Dreeben, 1968; Elkin and Handel, 1984; McLeod, 1987). Similarly, schools have rarely succeeded in educating their lower-class students to the same extent as those from the middle and upper classes (Katz, 1987). I will suggest that OSRP's ideological practice of silencing negative voice, ignoring barriers, and blaming failure on individuals does not encourage the adequate socialization of their students. Seen in this way, different social institutions are acting together to limit the life chances of these youngsters, even though their incumbents would not perceive it that way .

CONTRADICTIONS WITHIN OSRP

There are several contradictions within OSRP that explain why the program fails to have more of a positive impact upon the life chances of its students. These include OSRP's perception of its students, its rejection of lower-class culture, its relationship to work and to its own students, and its practices of silencing critical student voice and of ignoring barriers to upward mobility. I will examine these in turn.

First, consider the issue that the program ideology encourages the staff to perceive their students and families as deficient. This is diametrically opposed to the hopeful part of that same ideology. Hope requires a feeling that the students are capable and energetic enough to take advantage of available opportunities. There is a contradiction within OSRP because the program argues on the one hand for optimism and hope, while acknowledging on the other hand the unlikely nature of that possibility because of deficiencies. It is a truism that perceptions shape our relationships with each other: we tend to act toward others as we define them to ourselves (Hollander and Hunt, 1967). As such, we would not expect a staff who define their students in terms of their deficiencies to create a curriculum in practice that pressures and encourages their students to overcome their lifelong academic and social limitations. This is the power of the definition of the situation and of the other. Seen in this way, then, the program's very perception of its students contributes to its lack of success.

Second, OSRP fails to successfully reintegrate its students because it implicitly asks them to dislike themselves and their own lower-class and/or minority culture. The staff preach the virtues of upward mobility, trying to create an environment where that might occur. At the same time, however, they are asking their students to reject their social origins and replace them with something "better," that is, to implicitly view themselves and those they love as deficient. The staff do not intend their ideology as a denigration of students and parents; yet one must admit the possibility that many students intuitively understand this logical connection. From this perspective, it is not surprising that the students reject this ideology in their behaviors (if not in their spoken words).

Third, a disjunction exists between OSRP's official ideology and its students' work habits. The formal curriculum states that the program seeks to instill good work habits so that students can transfer those to the school and eventually to the occupational realm. Yet the students view OSRP work as trivial and unchallenging.

As a result, they do it without personal commitment. The staff want to prepare their students for a better future, but their inability to assign meaningful work manifests itself in staff and student apathy. Few of these young people come away understanding that work can add meaning to one's life and can help give one identity and self-direction. As Bowles and Gintis (1976) and Anyon (1981) predict, work continues to be defined within this program serving lower-class youth as an activity engaged in when someone is commanded to do so by another. Under these circumstances, one sees how little of it one can do.

I found that the staff care about these young people, but this type of caring is distorted by their tendency to take on a substitute parenting role. Elsewhere, I have called this "institutional caring" (Hamovitch, 1995). This occurs when middle-class professionals show concern for lower-class clients within an institutional context. This caring relationship has one of the parties being paid by a state agency to relate to or care for the other, who is defined in one or more critical ways as being in need or deficient. These relationships are likely to be one-sided in the sense that one party to the relationship is much more likely than the other to be perceived as being in charge or being advantaged in important ways. This often precludes the establishment of two-way patterns of speaking and listening that are integral to a caring relationship (Noddings, 1992). Only one party to the relationship has the perceived authority to enter into the private domain of the other. As this study has demonstrated, the caring by staff is a solution that often brings about its own problems, leading to resistance from those who are cared for. As such, these relationships can contradict their intent of supporting and encouraging the disadvantaged.

There is also a contradiction in OSRP's relationship to schools. Chapter 6 outlined a tirade of student critiques of these institutions, some of which bubble to the surface when the students come into the OSRP classroom after school. And yet I never observed any OSRP staff members legitimizing student critique by supporting its voice. Given the close cooperation and overlap in staff between OSRP and the schools, this is hardly surprising. Yet, it is also unexpected. Despite its apparent consistency with the program's purpose of assisting the integration of these young people within their schools, the failure to permit or encourage student critique seems to have the unintended consequence of acting against that central purpose of the program. The staff know that virtually all of their students are alienated from their schools. Yet, how do they expect to remedy the relations between these young people and their schools if the students are not given the latitude to discuss their grievances in an atmosphere of mutual respect and support? While I recognize that staff would respond that permitting or encouraging student voicing of critique might only further alienate students from their schools, it is clear that the present strategy of silencing is not working. Perhaps an admission that schools are not always adequately meeting these needs is far too personally threatening to middle-class adults who have benefited personally from that system. Yet these findings appear to indicate that OSRP's strategy of silencing critique contributes to its own failure. Students might benefit from having the opportunity to voice their antischool sentiments and experiences in a program staffed by adults who do not deny student anger, but rather help them turn their feelings into constructive action that is not solely individualistic.

Some would argue that as unsuccessful as OSRP's approach has been found to be, it is still likely to yield more upward social mobility than an alternative program that might encourage student critique of social institutions. For example, OSRP staff fear that their students would use critique as a crutch, further resigning them to their status as failures. In assessing this question, one must ask about socialization in general: how effectively can anyone hope to socialize others without actively listening to their voices? If students have deeply felt critiques about adult-run institutions, is it reasonable to expect to create and reinforce an ideology of hope without dealing openly with existing perceptions? If students intuitively understand something that they do not speak of, that is, that significant barriers impede their success, can we expect that silencing these will provide fertile ground for the growth of a more positive ideology? It is irrelevant to the students why OSRP minimizes barriers and silences student critique. Staff may be ignorant of the existence of barriers and/or they may be seeking to conceal them because of a belief that this is acting in the students' best interest. In either case a wide disjunction remains between expressed student and staff perceptions, making resocialization problematic.

Chapter 3 revealed that OSRP students hold naive understandings about the relationship between their current track placement and the potential for them to achieve their stated career aspirations. Yet, I often heard the staff support them in their naiveté. I suspect that part of this staff "innocence" is genuine, while another part is a deliberate attempt to mislead the students. In trying to understand this misdirection, it should be recalled that the staff see their role as needing to be positive about social institutions, thus encouraging the students to achieve within them. The staff fear that permitting negative ideas to predominate would be detrimental to students. Early in the course of the program, the staff ask the students to state a career aspiration, encouraging them to aspire as high as they can. The staff deliberately choose to elevate the students' aspirations and do not draw their attention to educational barriers. Is allowing these young people to think that they might one day become doctors or lawyers a cruel hoax or is it a reasonable strategy under the circumstances?

I observed that many OSRP students appear to take these high career aspirations seriously. The staff excite these young people about climbing toward the top of society's system of stratification in the hope that this might motivate them to do better in school. In part, they do this by denying the importance of tracking as a barrier to upward mobility. And yet research indicates that the chances of these children realizing their high aspirations are remote (see for example Coleman et al., 1966; Fine, 1991; Rist, 1973; Willis, 1977). Inevitably, most of these young people will experience the harsh reality of scholastic and other barriers. Stevenson and Ellsworth (1993) have demonstrated that when they fail to overcome these barriers, they are likely to react with self-blame. As a society, we seem unable to squarely face the contradiction that we want schools to be stratifying institutions at the same time that we desire that they create equalizing opportunities. The result is a tendency to be secretive about stratifying practices because schools do not wish to be seen as reducing equality of opportunity. Thus, it is not surprising that OSRP staff do not communicate a clear picture of the school's role in our stratification system.

The staff were also found to deny the existence of class, race, and gender barriers. Judging from OSRP students' inability to speak about these hurdles, the staff have been successful in inculcating the program's official ideology. I would argue, however, that the denial of classism, racism, and sexism is in contradiction of the research cited in chapter 1. The disjunction between the staff's idyllic world and the one lived by these students is overwhelming. OSRP students know from lived experience that class, race, and gender are statuses that influence how people interact with each other. It seems that staff denial of this disjunction only helps to reinforce the program's lack of relevance to these young people.

On the other hand, the program can be seen to be successful in inculcating its conservative ideology of hope. Students speak of having personal aspirations to achieve middle-class occupations, apparently believing that educational and economic institutions are open to them. The difficulty with this success is that all indications point in the direction of it being short-lived. The future is likely to bring self-blame when goals are not realized. This predictable pattern of self-blame has the effect of deflecting the possible condemning of institutional classism, racism, and sexism. Some might argue that this is a latent reward to offset state expenses for funding OSRP.

Above, I have explored a number of contradictions between OSRP goals and the curriculum in practice. Program staff demand a very low intensity of work and work commitment, they relate to their students as substitute parents, they minimize legitimate grievances that the students have with the school system, and they ignore class and other barriers. It has been argued that the effect of these has been to contradict OSRP's goal of successfully reintegrating its students into schools. Despite the fact that OSRP staff view their students as deficient, they honestly feel that their work helps to meet the present and future interests of these young people. Yet, they are limited by the program ideology and by their own perceptions and practices. These do not permit them to represent the long-term interests of OSRP students because these understandings lead to program policies and practices that contradict those very interests.

I believe that permitting the expression of critical perceptions of social institutions within OSRP would better represent the interests of at-risk young people. Stevenson and Ellsworth (1993) found that high school dropouts internalize society's image of their deficiency and silence their own criticisms of social institutions. Alternatively, an environment that permits the expression of critique might encourage the recognition of collective interests and the development of more useful explanations for some students' precarious educational, economic, and social position. Venting anger with social institutions might encourage constructive action rather than self-doubt and self-blame. Collective identities might develop, possibly leading to organizing and pressuring the political system for changes that at-risk students and their parents see as being in their best interest. In addition, pressure from the community might encourage some school personnel to join a lobby for reform that might equalize opportunity within schools for diverse groups of youngsters.

The notion that diverse groups within schools (and societies) have coinciding interests, values, and beliefs is built on hope more than observation. Administrators, teachers, and the "good" students are well served by this conservative ideology of hope: they have a lot to be hopeful about. The system responds to who they are, serving their needs comparatively well. But the ideology of hope does not meet the interests of less privileged students who do not integrate effectively and cooperatively into schools. Socialization efforts that ignore key problems through such methods as the silencing of voice and the reification of existing institutions are likely to end in failure. Ideological issues must be confronted if we are to extend a useful helping hand to at-risk students.

The idea that middle-class adults can take young people aside and "fix their thinking" so that at-risk students can learn to act like them and become successful like them is put in doubt by this study. Despite the talents and sincere efforts of OSRP staff, this strategy simply does not work. It is suggested here that this is the case because the program and its staff are trapped inside an ideological perspective that makes it difficult to genuinely respect the students' differences. The staff display outward signs of courtesy and caring toward their students, and yet hold them in low esteem. Although I believe that most of the staff do not consciously understand that their feelings toward these young people and their parents are negative, they do not respect their values, their intelligence, the choices that they make in life, and so forth. The program ideology does not encourage them to think otherwise.

Like Giroux (1989) I am inviting an alternative perspective that truly recognizes and appreciates difference. This means that institutions must be pressured by struggles from within and without to legitimate the cultural capital of disenfranchised groups. This perspective rejects the desirability of reaching out for unity within institutions. This study has allowed us to observe OSRP staff who are attempting to help their students out of a cycle of poverty. It is disconcerting that these staff cannot permit the expression of this group's victimization in terms that encourage them to recognize their collective relationships with state institutions (like public schools) or to collectively do something about the imbalance in those relationships.

IDEOLOGY AND SCHOOL FAILURE

Others have posited that society promulgates an ideology that is consistent with and exists logically prior to the one found among OSRP staff, students, and parents (see Berger, 1963; Berger and Luckmann, 1967; Mills, 1956). Detailed theoretical discussion of the precise nature of this ideology's relationship to material or structural conditions is outside the boundary of this research. However, I believe that it is not accidental that this set of ideas acts to legitimate the social and economic success of the wealthy. The central tenets of this ideology do not stand on their own in isolation from material interests of groups that control the dissemination of ideas through the media and other institutions. In fact, ideas serve as a source of legitimation for institutional arrangements that advantage the most powerful elements in society.

This study finds a congruity between the staff's and parents' ideological beliefs. Both see the program as manifesting their hope that the students may benefit individually from a belief in the openness of their society. They share the hope that if the young people in the program could only see the opportunities that are open and available to them, they would reorient themselves in relation to their schoolwork. The congruity of view of these two groups with their varying class, gender, and racial origins shows the pervasiveness of the achievement ideology within U.S. society.

It is interesting that the African American parents express such a positive and optimistic orientation to education as the main means of upward mobility for their children. In contrast, I found the Caucasian parents to be more hesitant about predicting that their children would experience success within the school system. This is surprising, in light of the fact that the African American parents are acutely aware of the presence of racism within their community schools and their society in general. However, this finding is consistent with Ogbu's (1988) finding that African American parents give their children mixed messages, viewing schooling as *the* means of upward mobility at the same time that they critique the society's tendency to exclude blacks instrumentally (economically) and expressively (socially). Ogbu argues that historically African Americans collectively struggled to gain educational access and achievement in the face of white exclusion. And yet the long history of conflict between African Americans and public schools has created a culture of distrust of these institutions within the African American community, which is also communicated to children at a young age. The result is the development of a mixed oppositional identity and culture that leaves African American children seeking success within the education system at the same time that they resist it. This is the paradoxical situation that Weis found in her (1985) study of Urban Community College. It is also consistent with Carnoy's (1989) conclusion that subordinate groups resist mainstream ideology, and with McCarthy's (1988) thesis that individuals and groups often react differently (and yet rationally) to objectively similar circumstances, interpreting their interests in ways that may seem unconventional. In the case of OSRP parents, it would not necessarily have been predictable that the African Americans would have been more optimistic than the Caucasians about their children's future success in school. This is because relationships between groups and institutions are complex, often defying commonly understood generalizations.

As I see it, OSRP's African American parents do not have the luxury of imagining any other ways for their children to achieve success within what they view as a racist society. Because of this perspective, they consciously attempt to inculcate their children with a belief in the idea that schools are the only route to upward mobility. This may be because educational institutions at least offer the guise of being meritocratic, extending legitimate opportunity to some African American children. In contrast, the Caucasian parents know their own personal failure at school, as well as that of their children. Unlike African Americans, they do not have the advantage of blaming the society for these failures, and so end up turning blame inward upon themselves and their children. They have no buffer (in the form of a racial identity) between themselves and the full weight of the dominant society that holds them in low esteem. They are more likely to experience their failures personally. For these reasons, and because they see their children turning out much like themselves, they become hesitant to postulate the success of their children. In short, despite (or perhaps because of) their white skin, they are less optimistic about their children's future place within the stratification system.

Despite the finding of some parental mixed messages and concerns about outcomes, the students are the recipients of a near-universal set of ideas from adults around them that describe their society's system of social stratification. Their schools, their after-school program (OSRP), and their parents sing the same chorus: aspire as high as you can, work hard in school, seize opportunities as they present themselves, and you will be rewarded economically and socially. This unanimity encourages the students to accept (or to at least voice their acceptance of) these ideas. In interaction with adults, they express their aspirations to high status occupations, recognize the need for schooling, and minimize any barriers that they might meet along the way. They project an image of a benign society filled with opportunity and devoid of barriers. Given students' spoken view of society and their high aspirations, one might ask why these young people continue to fail in school. I will cautiously offer four explanations based on the findings of this study, and aided by some of the findings and theoretical arguments of Weis and Ogbu. These explanations are divided into the following areas: the experience of the schools; the home and neighborhood cultures; unex-pressed doubts about the validity of the conservative ideology of hope; and the experience of OSRP.

From the evidence presented in this study, it should be clear that neither the program nor its ideology have the power to alter the conditions of (or the experience of) school for these young people. The conservative ideology of hope may be subjectively understood by the students to have validity, but its impact seems to diminish markedly within the school context. The school is understood by OSRP students as presenting alienating work and relations with adults. Weis (1985, 1990) found that there is a disjunction between the school curriculum and the culture of lower- and working-class students. For example, writing and speaking in standard English is the expected norm within schools, as is the use of a middle-class conception of time. OSRP students have deficiencies in the above areas that are not being compensated for within the program. They sense (but do not express) that it is somebody else's culture that is being endorsed in school. This is evidenced by the fact that they perceive school staff as not caring, not respecting students, and/or being racist. Like Weis's Urban Community College, there is a gulf between these students and their teachers. Since OSRP fails to confront the barriers between students and their schools directly, the young people remain on their own in deciding how to relate to those institutions on a day-to-day basis. The program ideology only offers conformism as a guide to daily experiences of alienation within schools, making it largely irrelevant to OSRP students. The predictable results, then, are the resistance, socializing, and failure that OSRP students told me characterize their activities at school.

The second reason why OSRP students fail in school despite their spoken belief in the program ideology is that their lower-class and African American cultures contain double messages concerning the validity of this ideology. It is significant that a difference exists between the African American and the Caucasian adolescents in the degree to which they adhere to this set of ideas. Although virtually all of the African American adolescents wholeheartedly concur with this ideology, a significant minority of the Springfield youth hold an alternative position. Stated sociologically, the alternative group's belief is that nonmeritocratic criteria are used within schools and within the occupational structure in determining success. This apparently surprising difference between African Americans and Caucasians corresponds to the dissimilarity noted above between the African American and Caucasian parents on the issue of whether or not they feel that their children can make the school system work for them in realizing their career aspirations. The feelings of doubt expressed by the Caucasian parents are also articulated by some of their children. They explain that their schools are inequitable, that nonschool criteria are factors in school success, and that they do not live in a fair society. This interpretation leads some of the Springfield group to feel that a rejection of school does not need to ensure their lack of social mobility. Since they perceive that they can get ahead without schooling, school failure is interpreted as just a temporary setback that is not really of much relevance in determining their future.

My speculation on why this divergence exists between African American and some white youngsters mirrors that of the above parental discussion. It is possible that the African American adolescents lack the feeling of security that there are alternative institutions (other than schools) within which they will be accepted and encouraged to achieve upward mobility based on their own interests, hard work, and talent. This is supported by Ogbu's (1978) finding of a historical job ceiling for African Americans, the remnants of which society is still experiencing. It is possible that the perception of a job ceiling could reinforce some poor African Americans' perception that the only route to upward mobility is by expressly following society's ideological commitment to education as the great equalizer. By contrast, some poor, at-risk Caucasian students comprehend that society's dominant economic institutions are controlled by others who look like themselves. This may give them the feeling that they may successfully enter and negotiate a place in the economy without relying exclusively on schooling. In this way, some poor Caucasian students interpret their present school failure as a tolerable situation.

The finding that African American OSRP students are unable to recognize barriers to upward mobility tends to refute Ogbu's job ceiling hypothesis. He argues that African American youth understand the existence of limited opportunities for themselves, and so give up trying to succeed within school. Ogbu may have found the objective existence of a job ceiling, but I found no evidence that lower-class River City African American students acknowledge that objective reality. Weis (1990) is particularly instructive on the issue of lower-class African American students' belief in the dominant ideology of schooling at the same time that they fail to follow through in practice within the school context. She finds a culture clash between the ghetto neighborhood and the school, arguing that this clash operates at the parental and peer group levels to mitigate against school success. For African American youngsters, the desire for success within the dominant culture leads to a contradiction. Dominant culture is white, and an open endorsement of this culture by African American youngsters is interpreted within the neighborhood as being a rejection of their shared culture. Weis found that the few African Americans who were successful at Urban Community College had to suffer the rejection of their peers, more or less "going it alone." Even though I presented no data to this effect, I found that one extremely articulate African American boy within OSRP (Wateef) followed this pattern, suffering the ridicule of being called an "Oreo" by OSRP students and staff. My observations support Weis's explanation of black students' conformity to the ideology of schooling at the same time that they reject the school as a dominant or white institution. Given this identification of schooling with whiteness, it is not surprising that school success is rather elusive to lower-class OSRP African American youth (despite the fact that they appear to believe in the conservative ideology of hope more so than their Caucasian counterparts).

Another reason for the disjunction between OSRP students' belief in the conservative ideology and their school failure lies in my feeling that some of their spoken beliefs are just that: expressed opinions rather than deeply held convictions. So many of their day-to-day behaviors in and out of school openly contradict their articulated ideology that it is hard to conclude that its main tenets are deep seated. Parents, OSRP staff, and other adults are unanimous in presenting this dominant ideology to these young people as an inspiration to elicit the response of voluntary school conformity. However, this ideology does little to speak directly to the alienation these lower class youth feel on a daily basis within schools. The development of socializing and resisting peer groups is evidence of this alienation. Weis (1990) found that the African American peer culture in Urban Community College does not contain within it any integrated set of ideas that contradict the achievement ideology, despite its behavioral rejection of that dominant ideology. Similarly, Stevenson and Ellsworth (1993) found that white dropouts are not part of an oppositional culture that expresses an ideology of resistance or critique of social institutions. Both studies conclude that the potential collective consciousness based on school failure, spoken critique of schools, and resistance to those institutions is truncated by the dominant ideology of schooling. Students are found to express a belief in schooling at the same time that they express other critiques and operate in a failed or failing mode. It is not unusual, then, for young people to mouth the words and ideas of adults at the same time that their behaviors and other expressed ideas point to disbelief. I postulate that this is what I found in OSRP. The young people lack a framework within which to question the dominant ideology, and so they speak the only words that they know. They possess many contradictory impulses based on their own experiences. But since they lack a coherent language of critique, they compartmentalize their alienation from school when they are asked to speak about such things as mobility, aspirations, and the nature of our stratification system. Thus, their spoken words sound a lot more like a single-minded belief in the ideology of hope than is really the case.

The young people react to OSRP in contradictory ways. They understand and respect the program's role in helping them set their career aspirations, giving them job experience, and assisting them with job skills. They maintain and augment their stated belief in the conservative ideology of hope. Alternatively, I found that OSRP students resist the day-to-day work that makes up the core of the program. Their resistance takes a variety of forms: they sit and wait to be told what to do at their job-trailings, they pay attention to the form (not the substance) of work requests, they are bored by the "thin" OSRP classroom assignments, and their classroom behavior can often be seen as "chaotic." Most, by their own admission, are in the program primarily to be paid. Thus, they experience nothing in OSRP that roughly replicates the meaning that work has to those high status members of the community whom they say they aspire to become. Work is experienced as something adults direct you to do, to which you respond sporadically and minimally, involving only part of your self.

Both the school and OSRP offer these students a similarly alienating relationship to work. As such, I do not believe that OSRP causes their academic failure. It is merely a lost opportunity to experience a more satisfying relationship to work. OSRP lacks the kind of experiential self-involvement that might be carried out of the program and into one's life (including the school classroom). It fails to convert its conservative ideological fervor into a set of experiences that might have the desired effect.

It is an anomaly that these young people emerge from OSRP genuinely believing in this conservative ideology of hope, and yet failing to act out the logical conse-quences of it within their schools. Any ideology is by definition a simplification of the part of the world that it is attempting to describe. This particular ideology, however, is clearly shaped by political considerations. In ignoring much of the research cited in the first chapter of this study, it posits a one-sided view of our stratification system that legitimates the status quo. While it theoretically offers hope to the young people in this study, it does so by describing an imaginary reality. Thus, the program misses an opportunity to give the students a time and place to express themselves, to touch base with sympathetic adults who will listen and help place their ideas within a variety of perspectives. By implication, the program ideology blames the very people whom it is attempting to serve.

A final factor that helps us understand OSRP students' school failure is their relationship with their own spoken aspirations. Every OSRP student is able to articulate a high status career aspiration on demand. Yet the automatic nature of their responses makes me suspect that they subjectively understand that being a doctor or a lawyer is not a realistic aspiration for them. They cannot really see themselves occupying those lofty positions in the future. They do not have a clear image of themselves in those roles partly because they have limited association with successful, middle-class adults. As a result, they lack an intimate understanding of what it is like to actually become whom they aspire. I believe that they subjectively understand those jobs as belonging to others, not them. As such, they do not have a vested interest in enduring the drudgeries of the schooling process. They lack a confidence that they will be paid back by actually achieving their career aspirations. Thus, despite OSRP's best intentions, its focus on career aspirations and improving self-esteem seems destined to failure.

The above comments should not be interpreted as adding to the victims' burden by blaming OSRP families for failing to provide role models of successful adults. In fact, I see marginal and powerless people as lacking resources to attain the satisfaction of their desires generally. The schooling of their children is just one important example of a more general phenomenon. Since Americans live in class-based neighborhoods and generally associate with others in similar economic positions, disadvantaged parents do not have ready access to relationships that might reverse the social isolation of themselves and their children. They did not create the class structure that limits their children's experiences. Lower-class parents do not enjoy the leverage that middle-class professionals take for granted. Social and economic structures abound that have the effect of telling the poor that they are not entitled to what others have. Experience teaches them that they and their children have good reason to be uncertain about the future.

PRACTICAL IMPLICATIONS

This final section will explore some of the implications of the findings of this research. Many of the implications have already been noted by prior researchers, and these will be acknowledged whenever I am aware of them. My focus will be on areas where the study can make a contribution to our thinking about practical action.

One logical implication of this study focuses on a concern over curriculum. Goodlad (1984), Cornbleth (1990), Page (1991), Fine and Rosenberg (1983), and Fine (1986, 1989) argue from their own research that curriculum needs serious attention for several reasons, not the least of which is student alienation from school. For example, Fine argues that many students leave school at least partly because the experiences and histories of others like them are ignored by the curriculum. These researchers propose changing the standard curriculum to reflect the lived experience of all students, including those who are presently disenfranchised. I concur that OSRP students are experiencing the same alienation found by these researchers, and that much of it is no doubt related to the lack of relevance of the school curriculum to their lived experience. OSRP students' critiques reveal a feeling that class time can be torturous. Educators may be able to persuade many students to acknowledge the legitimacy of their course work, but those without the same degree of vested interest will balk from the demand to engage with an alien curriculum.

Second, this study implies a need to rethink typical school organizational practices that constrain relationships between students and teachers. Cusick (1973) seems to be talking on behalf of OSRP students when he argues that high schools structure themselves in such a manner that they allow almost no time for students and teachers to interact outside of large group settings. According to Cusick, this allows students to remain more or less on their own, without adult guidance or pressure. This idea relates directly to the teachers do not care and teachers do not respect students themes articulated in chapter 6. If teachers and students had structured opportunities to interact individually and in small groups, this would no doubt help change the us versus them definitions that are implicit in OSRP students' descriptions of their relationships with teachers. Where there is a lack of close communication between groups, they can continue to stereotype and objectify each other without fear of having to confront complexity. Thus, initiatives should be taken within schools to encourage the evolution of student-teacher relations along the lines suggested here.

Third, these findings add a dimension of caution to those who would advocate a "caring" model. Successful relationships are not simply a matter of caring or not caring. On a personal level, OSRP staff are genuinely concerned about the students in their program, but this interest offers the potential for certain problems to surface in the relationship between young people, their parents, and staff. As Noddings (1992) seems to predict, OSRP staff act as though they wish their students could become "just like them." They see themselves as a counterweight to the deficient socialization practices of parents. This makes conflict over their advice and guidance of young people inevitable. In OSRP, it is the young people who are often caught in the middle between opposing forces. My observations reveal that OSRP students had more allegiance to the cultural scripts of their families and friends than to the moral advice-giving of staff persons. This is likely the case because the students sense that the caring that staff offer is only fleeting, being confined to a role that is limited in duration and depth.

If we are generally agreed that caring by professional staff is superior to noncaring, this study might suggest to some that what is needed are more critically perceptive staff members who do not blame students and their parents for their own failure. One might argue that staff need to start out with a genuine respect (not just a spoken respect) for their students before they can begin to relate to them in a truly caring fashion. Similarly, educators working with lower-class, at-risk youth should consider conducting themselves in concert with parents, not in direction of them. Together, adults could strive for genuine understandings of what they are attempting to accomplish together, rather than as one group attempting to compete with or dominate the other.

Further, one might suggest that a solution to these problems lies in encouraging staff not to be judgmental in relation to their students. It is conceivable that if teachers were more aware of how they are silently perceived by their students, they could alter their attitudes and behaviors in relation to them. Yet, the problem remains about how to achieve a goal such as establishing truly caring relationships between students and teachers. The fact that institutional caring is pervasive across a broad spectrum of contexts (Gans, 1962; Ogbu, 1974; Miller, 1991) suggests that this phenomenon is not personal or individual, but rather structural, in nature. Individualistic solutions to a structural problem are unlikely to meet with success. That is why responses that invite a quick fix (such as teacher sensitivity training) are less likely to affect real change than others that look for the structural roots of relationship difficulties.

In addition, this study shows that the solution to noncaring environments cannot be bought with money. If OSRP's 4.6:1 student-staff ratio cannot buy reciprocal caring, it appears that funding alone is not the answer. That being said, however, current school funding levels do not seem to permit professional staff to have an intimate knowledge of each child. One might argue that knowledge of students' lived experiences drops off sharply as social class differences between the teacher and the student widen. Schools serving lower-class and minority youth are often staffed by teachers and other professionals who are forced to operate on their own superficial understandings based on limited observation, partial communication with students, stereotypic perceptions of race and social class, and limited contact with parents. These teacher deficits are reinforced by organizational practices within schools. I leave it to the reader to think of creative ways to increase genuine reciprocal communication between teachers, students, and parents.

Another implication of this study concerns the relationship between young people and staff members of adult-run programs, whether they be within or outside of schools. In my experience, staff generally feel that they best know the young people in their care, as well as how they can meet their needs. However, the findings of this study suggest that the understandings that staff develop of the young people in their care are only partial. This research reveals that there are important thoughts and experiences that young people keep private from professional adults who supervise them. This is understandable, in light of the fact that staff hold authority over them (hence, the revealing of certain things might be associated with negative repercussions). The quality of these relationships is also influenced by the fact that interactions usually occur within group contexts, often involving a crossing of social class or racial boundaries. These factors are not particularly conducive to the open interaction that staff are desirous of and often purposefully seek to encourage. In addition, this study finds that staff tend to emphasize the positive contributions that they make on behalf of young people, to the near exclusion of critical perceptions. I found that staff actions reflect their partial understandings, despite their best intentions. As such, it is inadvisable to accept one's partial knowledge as being in any way complete. Staff should recognize that there are significant gaps in their understandings of where their students are coming from, where they are going, and what their institution is in fact doing for them.

Fourth, I believe that OSRP students' naiveté concerning the repercussions of their nonacademic track placement is highly revealing. It exposes the fact that authorities do not openly reveal the role that schools play in credentialing for employers. The result is that tracking is carried out in a manner that does not ensure that all students and parents understand the consequences of track choice for life chances. Other research has documented serious consequences of the tracking system for nonacademic students (e.g., Ball, 1981; Furlong, 1985; Heyns, 1974; Oakes, 1985; Rist, 1973). This research, together with the finding of extreme naiveté on the part of OSRP students, suggests that changes in tracking policy must be considered by educators. Our schools should attempt to limit the number of students placed in tracks that disqualify them from making the widest possible range of life choices. And when tracking choices are made, they should involve complete disclosure to students and parents concerning the likely ramifications of those choices with respect to future participation in the economy.

A fifth implication of this study relates to my observation that OSRP students are given little opportunity to make decisions in relation to the program. Other researchers have found that there is an association between lack of decision making and boredom within schools (Squibb, 1975; Sizer, 1984; Cusick, 1973). Newmann (1981) discovered that student alienation could be reduced by allowing students to be more involved in making decisions within schools. He makes three suggestions in response to this problem: (1) schools should be developed to reflect shared values of students and their parents; (2) students should be given the opportunity to participate in the development of school policy and management; and (3) students should be given the opportunity to integrate curriculum with individual personality and experience. Participation in decision making implies commitment, and it is that latter quality that is lacking in many students' relations with their schools. I urge the reader to consider Newmann's suggestions and to imagine others that could truly democratize schools. Properly conceived and implemented, they would promote the reintegration of at-risk students within their schools.

A final implication for practice emanates from this study's finding that the prevailing conservative ideology of hope fails to represent the best interests of the at-risk school population. I suggest that students should be given space to closely examine that ideology and to consider alternative paradigms that also help interpret our system of stratification. Other researchers, such as Giroux (1989), Giroux and McLaren (1989), Gore (1990), and Willis (1977) have articulated a belief that a critical pedagogy should be taught within schools. Additional investigations (Fine, 1986, 1989; Stevenson and Ellsworth, 1993; Foster, 1990) suggest that educators should not passively accept the prevailing ideology that assumes that institutions are benign and that the unteachable are victims. I believe that pedagogies that invite a variety of interpretations of current social arrangements would assist all students (but particularly at-risk students) in their relationships with schools and other institutions. This would enable students to develop their own language of understanding. Using this, they could redefine known truths by comparing them to evidence, thus permitting victims to squarely confront their victimization.

It occurs to me that OSRP staff would respond to the above suggestion with concern that elucidating barriers and limited life chances might act to further alienate young people from schools. They would argue that their minimizing of barriers gives hope (even if it might be interpreted as being false hope). My response is that while there is logic to this reasoning, it is not a sensible approach to take with adolescents who are alienated from school. For one, it does not work. OSRP does not achieve its goals because it assumes that its students are living in a vacuum in which critique of social institutions does not occur. To the extent that some staff acknowledge the preexistence of critique, they operate under the assumption that somehow they have the ability to supersede those negative analyses picked up from other sources. My promotion of critique depends upon perceiving at-risk young people as capable of thoughtfully responding to critical ideas. I assume that they are capable of seriously considering issues that directly affect their social and economic well-being. OSRP staff might perceive their students as lacking in the ability to thoughtfully critique social institutions because of the young peoples' negative reaction to the existing curriculum in practice and because of their perception of them as deficient. Yet, it is clear that the students had very good reason to reject the thin and alienating OSRP curriculum. In contrast to the ideas of the staff, my impression is that the majority of OSRP students have the potential to focus and to think seriously about important issues that they perceive as being relevant to them. Thus, it would be a shame to peremptorily conclude that young people who are alienated from their schools are incapable of positively responding to a curriculum that includes critical explorations of their social world.

This study confirms the idea that a top-down, state-controlled program based on an individualistic model that places the blame on those who are the victims of institutional arrangements is not a good basis upon which to rehabilitate at-risk students. We must get away from a model that assumes that our society is fundamentally healthy, except for a minority who should be resocialized. OSRP students are considered to need program treatment. This perception comes dangerously close to a kind of class and racial colonization, making no effort to truly understand and then respond to the root causes of the students' difficulties with their schools. There is no quick fix of others' thinking that is going to work without substantially altering their economic and social experiences. Culture is intimately related to one's day-to-day life and cannot be altered without a recognition of that reality. Adjusting another's behavior so that it is more consistent with one's altruistic desires is not a simple process (nor would I say that it is a desirable process) to accomplish, irrespective of one's political orientation. It appears that culture is not something that one can give to another person, like a gift. One can only exercise one's power in an attempt to help others exercise their own (Gore, 1990). Solutions will likely be long term, taking the time to include grass-roots community political organization. The disadvantaged resist the middle class and state officials who think they know how they should change themselves. Perhaps this is as it should be.

Appendix: Methods

This appendix gives the reader additional information about how the data were gathered for this study. I will discuss the various methods that allowed me to gather the data, explain how I gained access to OSRP, and present some of my impressions about my relationships with subjects. In addition, I review how the subjects were selected to participate in the program, and give a brief overview of the two sites. Finally, I present a general statement indicating how I view the data-gathering and coding processes.

The data-gathering process was largely completed by following the advice and guidance in qualitative methodology described by Bogdan and Biklen (1992). The focus in this methodology is on inductive analysis, description, and subjects' perceptions. The emphasis is on discovering the varieties of realities that are present in a complex group situation. Research is approached inductively, with a set of loosely framed questions. This allows the researcher to remain flexible in responding to serendipitous leads and findings. It permits the research to take on new directions as one progresses through the process of data collection and analysis. For example, the focus of this study changed from its original concentration on the relationship between the students and their schools to one that ultimately focused on an examination of OSRP's programmatic efforts.

The data are based on the participant observations (in which I functioned primarily as an observer) and semistructured interviews that were completed by myself during the months of January to July 1992. I attended and observed OSRP classroom sessions, job-trailing sites, and field trips. I conducted in-depth interviews with staff, students, parents, and job-trailing employers. Written program documents were gathered and analyzed as a further source of information. Generally, I attended three or four classroom sessions each week, in addition to interviews and job-trailing observations. Field notes were taken openly by myself during observations, followed by an expansion of these notes shortly thereafter (usually within a few hours). Casual encounters were also recorded in my notes as soon as practical.

Gaining access to OSRP was surprisingly easy. I had heard about the program from a friend whose relative is a staff member in the program. I sensed in talking to her that it would be an interesting site in which to conduct my research on at-risk students. I met with Gerald shortly thereafter, explained the nature of my research, and started observing within a few days. I believe that this process was eased by the fact that Gerald was also working on a graduate degree, making him sympathetic to my need to find a site at which to conduct my dissertation research.

All the staff and students agreed to allow me to interview them personally, although a complete acceptance was difficult to achieve with some subjects. For example, one staff member initially refused to allow me to tape-record our conversations, although we did spend many hours in discussion (during which I would take notes). Toward the end of the program, I earned his trust enough for him to permit a recording of a final interview. In addition, a student only allowed me to interview her once, at which point she declined future requests for individual interviews. She did, however, consent to participate in one of the small group interviews that I conducted with the students. She was one among a small number of the young people who could never quite understand why I would want to know things about them that they consider to be personal. By contrast, the vast majority of the students were cooperative and willing to put up with my observing, note taking, and questioning. Some would actively seek me out to tell me the latest news with respect to events in their own lives and the program. The adults that I interviewed seemed to have a category for researcher: they accepted my reason for being there as legitimate, and earnestly tried to assist me in my attempts to understand how OSRP functions.

Because my age is much more in line with that of the staff than the students, I had to be careful not to be seen to align myself with the staff. I neither directed nor assisted the students in their work, nor did I actually complete the work myself. My role as a nonparticipant observer was to attend, scrutinize, and ask people to help me with my understanding of ongoing events and practices. After a while, the staff (particularly Gerald) got so used to me being around that they would sometimes ask me to complete staff-type functions. I resisted this as much as possible, because I felt that it would interfere with the students' acceptance of me as a researcher. I did not wish them to identify me as a staff member, in fear that they might hold back ideas and experiences from me that they thought the staff might disapprove of. In the end, I only performed a small number of emergency-related functions as a surrogate staff person. For example, I agreed to drive the students on a field trip when no one else was available to complete this task.

One of the main methods that I utilized in data collection was in-depth interviewing of OSRP staff, the young people in the program, their parents, and their job-trailing supervisors. These interviews were audio recorded, transcribed, and analyzed. I used unstructured interviewing, employing open-ended questions. This has the potential to produce data that are rich in the detail that the subject himself or herself wishes to provide. In this type of interviewing, the researcher tries to be as nondirective as possible. The progression of these interviews is not always predictable in advance. When things go well, the researcher gains insight into the subject's frame of reference. He or she comes to understand how the subject views the world (or particular aspects thereof). Individuals have varying attention spans, degrees of oral fluency, and so forth, so the interviews varied significantly in length. The average interview with each of the thirty-three students and the eight staff lasted approximately one hour. The interviews with the parents and the employers typically took somewhat less time. Some of the students were interviewed on more than one occasion, and nearly all the staff had multiple interviews.

OSRP students had all been labeled as at risk by their schools. The process for admission into the program is as follows. Guidance counselors at the middle and high schools are all aware of the existence of the program, and encourage students on their roster to apply to the program. They understand that there is a financial qualification limiting entry to the program: each student's family income has to fall below the poverty line. Guidance counselors also comprehend that the student has to be at risk of dropping out of school for one reason or another, and would in their judgement likely benefit from the program. The guidance counselors interpret this to mean that the potential applicant is not a "lost cause."

From my observations, a very high percentage of those students who apply to the program and who financially qualify are admitted. There is some conscious effort to include a balance of males and females within each group. The Springfield groups have historically been Caucasian, due to the racial composition of the community (nonwhites represent 1.7 percent of the Springfield population). In contrast, the River City students have been overwhelmingly African American, despite the fact that this group makes up only 16 percent of the River City population. This reality has been explained to me in a variety of different ways, leading me to conclude that the following factors are of central importance. African American overrepresentation is likely related to the fact that the neighborhood in which the program is located is predominantly African American and poor. It is also attributable to the fact that the program initially developed with that racial imbalance, and there is resistance among whites to send their children to a program with a black majority membership. Last, it is likely that there is an overrepresentation of African Americans among students whom school staff would define as being at risk.

The subjects and the data were treated in a manner consistent with SUNY - Buffalo's ethical guidelines. This means that the subjects agreed to be part of the study voluntarily, understanding the nature of the study, potential risks, and obligations. Written parental consent of students was obtained, in addition to their own personal consent to be part of the study.

I saw the data collection process as being like a funnel that starts out wide at the top, and gradually narrows down to areas of concentration. Borrowing from Strauss (1987), I repeatedly found myself going through the stages of induction, deduction, and verification. Hunches frequently turned into tentative generalizations that in turn led to a process of verification, partial verification, or refutation. This was a continuous cycle that eventually resulted in provisional and eventually more permanent linkages between "discovered" concepts. After a few months in the field, it slowly became evident that the central concept would be the conservative ideology of hope. Its potential linkages to other concepts and findings were explored in memos to myself, pursuant to and followed by attempts at verification in the field.

The coding stage lasted two to three months. This was one of the most difficult work experiences that I have ever had. It was filled with personal doubts about my attempts to fairly represent my most important experiences and observations at OSRP. I started by reading and rereading all the collected documents, field notes, interviews, and memos, looking for coding categories that best recognize patterns that the data appeared to be expressing. With the help of a computer program (Seidel, Kjolseth and Seymour, 1988), coding categories were printed out and placed into files. Then the coded data were re-read and perused for interrelationships between categories. Some eliminating and redefining of coding categories occurred at this point. Finally, coded materials were established and placed into files. I then started the tedious process of writing summaries of each individual file. When this was complete, I briefly resummarized the summaries, and reexamined these for interrelationships between folders. This process represents a personal customizing of the analysis suggestions presented in chapter 5 of Bogdan and Biklen (1992). Slowly, the relationships and interrelationships that became the themes of this research came to the fore.

References

Abercrombie, N., Hill, S., & Turner, B. S. (1984). The Penguin dictionary of sociology (2nd ed.). London: Penguin Books.

Alexander, K., Cook, M., & McDill, E. L. (1978). Curriculum tracking and educational stratification: Some further evidence. *American Sociological Review, 79* (43), 47–66.

Althusser, L. (1972). Ideology and ideological state apparatusses. In B. R. Cosin (Ed.), *Education: Structure and society*. Harmondsworth, Middlesex: Penguin Books.

Anyon, J. (1981). Social class and school knowledge. *Curriculum Inquiry, 1* (1), 3–42.

———. (1995). Race, social class and educational reform in an inner-city school. *Teachers College Record, 97* (1), 69–94.

Apple, M. (1976). The hidden curriculum and the nature of conflict. In H. Strub, *The sociology of education*. Homewood, IL: The Dorsey Press.

Ball, S. (1981). *Beachside comprehensive*. Cambridge: Cambridge University Press.

Berger, P. L. (1963). *Invitation to sociology*. New York: Anchor Books.

Berger, P. L., & Luckmann, T. (1967). *The social construction of reality: A treatise in the sociology of knowledge*. New York: Anchor Books.

Bernstein, B. (1977). Social class, language and socialization. In J. Karabel and A. H. Halsey (Eds.), *Power and ideology in education* (pp. 473–486). New York: Oxford University Press.

Bloom, B. S., Davis, A., & Hess, R. (1965). *Compensatory education for cultural deprivation*. New York: Holt, Rinehart & Winston.

Bogdan, R. C., & Biklen, S. K. (1992). *Qualitative research for education: An introduction to theory and methods* (2nd ed.). Boston: Allyn and Bacon.

Bourdieu, P. (1977). Cultural reproduction and social reproduction. In J. Karabel and A. H. Halsey (Eds.), *Power and ideology in education* (pp. 487–511). New York: Oxford University Press.

Bowles, S., & Gintis, H. (1976). *Schooling in capitalist America*. New York: Basic Books.

Callahan, R. E. (1962). *Education and the cult of efficiency*. Chicago: University of Chicago Press.

Carnoy, M. (1975). Is compensatory education possible? In M. Carnoy (Ed.), *Schooling in a corporate society: The political economy of education in America* (2nd ed.). New York: David McKay.

———. (1989). Education, state, and culture in American society. In H. Giroux & P. McLaren (Eds.), *Critical pedagogy, the state and cultural struggle*. Albany: SUNY Press.

Coleman, J., Campbell, E., Hobson, C., McPartland, J., Mood, A., Weinfeld, F., & York, R. (1966). *Equality of educational opportunity*. Washington: U.S. Office of Education.

Collins, R. (1979). *The credential society: An historical sociology of education*. New York: Academic Press.

Cornbleth, C. (1990). *Curriculum in context*. London: Falmer Press.

Cummins, J. (1986). Empowering minority students: A framework for intervention. *Harvard Educational Review, 56* (1), 18–36.

Cusick, P. A. (1973). *Inside high school: The students' world*. New York: Holt, Rinehart and Winston.

Dreeben, R. (1968). *On what is learned in school*. Reading, MA: Addison Wesley Publishing.

Elkin, F., & Handel, G. (1984). *The child and society: The process of socialization* (4th ed.). New York: Random House.

Everhart, R. E. (1983). *Reading, writing and resistance: Adolescence and labor in a junior high school*. Boston: Routledge and Kegan Paul.

Fensham, P. (Ed.). (1986). *Alienation from schooling*. Melbourne; Boston: Routledge and Kegan Paul.

Fine, M. (1986). Why urban adolescents drop into and out of public high school. *Teachers College Record, 87* (3), 393–409.

———. (1987). Silencing in public schools. *Language Arts, 64* (2), 157–174.

———. (1989). Silencing and nurturing voice in an improbable context: Urban adolescents in public school. In H. A. Giroux & P. McLaren (Eds.), *Critical pedagogy, the state, and cultural struggle*. Albany: SUNY Press.

———. (1991). *Framing dropouts: Notes on the politics of an urban public high school*. Albany: SUNY Press.

Fine, M., & Rosenberg, P. (1983). Dropping out of high school: The ideology of school and work. *Journal of Education, 165* (3), 257–272.

Fordham, S. (1991). Peer-proofing academic competition among black adolescents: "Acting White" Black American style. In C. Sleeter (Ed.), *Empowerment through multicultural education*. Albany: SUNY Press.

Foster, M. (1990). The politics of race: Through African-American teachers' eyes. Paper presented at the annual meeting of the AERA, Boston, MA.

Freire, P. (1970). *Pedagogy of the oppressed*. New York: Herder and Herder.

———. (1973). *Education for critical consciousness*. New York: Continuum.

Frost, L. E. (1994). "At-risk" statuses: Defining deviance and suppressing difference in public schools. *Journal of Law and Education, 23* (2), 123–165.

Furlong, V. J. (1985). *The deviant pupil: Sociological perspectives*. Milton Keynes, England and Philadelphia: Open University Press.

Gabriel, R. M., & Rasp, A., Jr. (1986). Educating Washington's at-risk youth: A synthesis of policies and recent studies. Washington, DC: Washington Office of the Superintendent of Public Instruction.

Gans, H. J. (1962). *The urban villagers: Group and class in the life of Italian-Americans*. New York: The Free Press.

Gartner, A., & Riessman, F. (1993). Make sure helping helps. *Social Policy, 24* (1), 35–36.

Gartner, A., & Riessman, F. (1994). Tutoring helps those who give, those who receive. *Educational Leadership, 52* (3), 58–60.

Gibson, R. (1986). *Critical theory and education*. London: Hodder and Stroughton.

Ginsburg, M. B. (1988). *Contradictions in teacher education and society: A critical analysis*. London: Falmer Press.

Giroux, H. A. (1989). Schooling as a form of cultural politics: Toward a pedagogy of and for difference. In H. A. Giroux & P. McLaren (Eds.), *Critical pedagogy, the state, and cultural struggle* (pp.125–151). Albany, NY: SUNY Press.

Giroux, H. A., & McLaren, P. (1989). Schooling, cultural politics, and the struggle for democracy. In H. A. Giroux and P. McLaren (Eds.), *Critical pedagogy, the state, and cultural struggle* (pp. xi–xxxv). Albany: SUNY Press.

Goodlad, J. I. (1984). *A place called school: Prospects for the future.* New York: McGraw-Hill.

Gore, J. M. (1990). What can we do for you! What can "we" do for "you"?: Struggling over empowerment in critical and feminist pedagogy. *Educational Foundations, 4* (3), 5–26.

Gouldner, A. W. (1976). *The dialectic of ideology and technology: The origins, grammar, and future of ideology.* New York: Seabury Press.

Halsey, A. H. (1977). Towards meritocracy? The case of Britain. In J. Karabel & A. H. Halsey (Eds.), *Power and ideology in education.* New York: Oxford University Press.

Hamovitch, B. A. (1995). Caring in an institutional context: Can it really occur? *Educational Foundations, 9* (4), 25–39.

Heyns, B. (1974). Social selection and stratification within schools. *American Journal of Sociology, 79* (6), 1434–1451.

Hollander, E. P., & Hunt, R. G. (1967). Person perception, interaction, and role. In E. P. Hollander & R. G. Hunt (Eds.), *Current perspectives in social psychology* (2nd ed.). New York: Oxford University Press.

Hummel, R. C., & Nagel, J. M. (1975). The character of bureaucracy in urban schools. In H. R. Stub (Ed.), *The sociology of education: A sourcebook* (3rd ed.). Homewood, IL: Dorsey Press.

Jencks, C., Crouse, J., & Mueser, P. (1983). The Wisconsin model of status attainment: A national replication with improved measures of ability and aspiration. *Sociology of Education, 51* (January), 3–19.

Jencks, C., Smith, M., Acland, H., Bane, M., Cohen, D., Gintis, H., Heyns, B., & Michelson, S. (1972). *Inequality: A reassessment of the effect of family and schooling in America.* New York: Basic Books.

Katz, M. B. (1987). *Reconstructing American education.* Cambridge, MA: Harvard University Press.

Ladson-Billings, G., & Tate, W. F. (1995). Toward a critical race theory of education. *Teachers College Record, 97* (1), 47–68.

Lipset, S. M., & Bendix, R. (1966). *Social mobility in industrial society.* Berkley & Los Angeles: University of California Press.

Lortie, D. (1975). *Schoolteacher: A sociological study.* Chicago: University of Chicago Press.

MacLeod, J. (1987). *Ain't no makin' it: Leveled aspirations in a low-income neighborhood.* Boulder, CO: Westview Press.

McCarthy, C. (1988). Rethinking liberal and radical perspectives on racial inequality in schooling: Making the case for nonsynchrony. *Harvard Educational Review, 58* (3), 265–279.

McLaren, P. (1986). *Schooling as a ritual performance.* Boston: Routledge and Kegan Paul.

McNeil, L. M. (1988). *Contradictions of control: School structure and school knowledge.* New York: Routledge.

Miller, G. (1991). *Enforcing the work ethic: Rhetoric and everyday life in a work incentive program.* Albany: SUNY Press.

Mills, C. W. (1956). *The power elite.* New York: Oxford University Press.

Newmann, F. M. (1981). Reducing student alienation in high schools: Implications of theory. *Harvard Educational Review, 17* (4), 546–564.

Nisbet, R. (1952). Conservatism and sociology. *American Journal of Sociology, (62)* (September), 167–175.

Noddings, N. (1992). *The challenge to care in schools: An alternative approach to education.* New York: Teachers College Press.

Oakes, J. (1985). *Keeping track: How schools structure inequality.* Binghamton, NY: Vail-Ballou Press.

O'Brien, L. (1993). Issues in education: Is our two-tiered system of early care and education fair? *Childhood Education, 70* (1), 2–3.

Ogbu, J. (1974). *The next generation: An ethnography of education in an urban neighborhood.* New York: Academic Press.

———. (1978). *Minority education and caste: The American system in cross-cultural perspective.* New York: Academic Press.

———. (1988). Class, stratification, racial stratification, and schooling. In L. Weis (Ed.), *Class, race, and gender in American education.* Albany: SUNY Press.

Page, R. (1991). *Lower-track classrooms: A curricular and cultural perspective.* New York: Teachers College Press.

Parsons, T. (1954). A revised analytical approach to the theory of social stratification. In T. Parsons (Ed.), *Essays in sociological theory* (rev. ed.). New York: Free Press of Glencoe.

Powell, A. G., Farrar, E., & Cohen, D. K. (1985). *The shopping mall high school: Winners and losers in the educational marketplace.* Boston: Houghton Mifflin.

Ramey, C. T. (1992). High-risk children and I.Q: Altering intergenerational patterns. *Intelligence, 16,* 239–256.

Ramey, M., & Johnson, E. (1991). *Even start/project family program: First annual review.* ED 338 773.

Reyes, A. (1995). Funding at-risk compensatory programs: An urban high school case study. *The Urban Review, 27* (2), 141–158.

Rist, R. C. (1973). *The urban school: A factory for failure.* Cambridge: MIT Press.

Rosenbaum, J. E. (1976). *Making inequality: The hidden curriculum of high school tracking.* New York: John Wiley and Sons.

Rosenthal, R., & Jacobson, L. (1968). *Pygmalion in the classroom: Teacher expectation and pupils' intellectual development.* New York: Holt, Rinehart and Winston.

Rutter, M., Maughan, B., Mortimore, P., Ouston, J., & Smith, A. (1979). *Fifteen thousand hours: Secondary schools and effects on children.* Cambridge: Harvard University Press.

Ryan, W. (1971). *Blaming the victim.* New York: Pantheon Books.

Sedlak, M. W., Wheeler, C. W., Pullin, D. C., & Cusak, P. A. (1986). *Selling students short: Classroom bargains and academic reform in the American high school.* New York: Teachers College Press.

Seidel, J. V., Kjolseth, R., & Seymour, E. (1988). *The ethnograph.* Corvallis, OR: Qualis Research Associates.

Shujaa, M. (1993). Education and schooling: You can have one without the other. *Urban education, 27* (4), 328–351.

Sizer, T. R. (1984). *Horace's compromise: The dilemma of the American high school.* Boston: Houghton Mifflin.

Solomon, R. P. (1989). Dropping out of academics. In L. Weis, E. Farrar, & H. G. Petrie (Eds.), *Dropouts from school: Issues, dilemmas & solutions*. Albany: SUNY Press.

Squibb, P. G. (1975). Education and class. In H. R. Stub (Ed.), *The sociology of education*. London: Dorsey Press.

Stevenson, R. B., & Ellsworth, J. (1993). Dropouts and the silencing of critical voices. In L. Weis & M. Fine (Eds.), *Beyond silenced voices: Class, race, and gender in United States schools*. Albany: SUNY Press.

Strauss, A. L. (1987). *Qualitative analysis for social scientists*. Cambridge: Cambridge University Press.

Tripp, D. (1986). Greenfield: A case study of schooling, alienation and employment. In P. Fensham (Ed.), *Alienation from schooling*. London: Kegan Paul.

Tyack, D. B. (1974). *The one best system: A history of American urban education*. Cambridge, MA: Harvard University Press.

U.S. Department of Education (1993). *Summer challenge: Model summer programs for disadvantaged students*. Washington, DC: U.S. Government Printing Office.

Wehlage, G. G., Rutter, R. A., Smith, G. A., Lesko, N., & Fernandez, R. R. (1989). *Reducing the risk: Schools and communities of support*. London and New York: Falmer Press.

Weis, L. (1985). *Between two worlds: Black students in an urban community college*. Boston: Routledge & Kegan Paul.

————. (1990). *Working class without work: High school students in a de-industrializing economy*. New York: Routledge, Chapman and Hall.

Whyte, W. F. (1943). *Street corner society*. Chicago: University of Chicago Press.

Williams, S. B. (1987). A comparative study of black dropouts and black high school graduates in an urban public school system. *Education and Urban Society, 19* (3), 311–319.

Willis, P. (1977). *Learning to labor: How working class kids get working class jobs*. New York: Columbia University Press.

Woods, P. (1990). *The happiest days?: How pupils cope with school*. London and Philadelphia: Falmer Press.

Wright, C. (1986). School processes: An ethnographic study. In J. Eggleson, D. Dunn, & M. Anjali (Eds.), *Education for some: The educational and vocational experiences of 15–18 year old members of minority ethnic groups*. Stoke on Trent: Trentham Books.

————. (1987). The relations between teachers and Afro-Carribean pupils: Observing multiracial classrooms. In G. Weiner & M. Arnot (Eds.), *Gender under scrutiny: New inquiries in education*. London: Hutchinson, in association with the Open University.

Index

Ability grouping. *See* Tracking
African American schools, 98, 102
Alienated students, 3-5, 17, 113, 115, 117, 119
Aspirations, student, 12, 17, 19-21, 26, 28, 30, 106, 109-10, 113-16
At-risk students, 3-5, 10-15, 70-71, 84, 99-101, 105, 110-11, 118-20

Barbara, 54, 63-64
Barriers to mobility, 39-4-, 47, 53, 56-57, 59-61, 105-10, 113-14, 120
Blaming the system, 59

Career aspirations, 12, 17, 19-21, 26, 28, 106, 109-10, 113-16
Career training, 28
Caring, 5, 26, 53, 55-56, 84, 117-18; of OSRP staff, 48, 50, 69, 80-81, 83-84, 108, 111; of teachers, 88, 93-95, 98, 101, 105, 113; of parents, 71, 74, 77, 79, 81-82
College trip, 30-31
Compensatory education, 1-3, 8, 13, 32
Conservative ideology of hope, 7, 32, 35-36, 41-45, 50-51, 53, 67-69, 84, 87, 103, 106, 110, 113, 115-16, 120, 125
Contradictions within OSRP, 83, 107-10
Cornbleth, Catherine, 4, 117
Counseling, 20, 30-2, 56-58, 66-67, 79
Critique of institutions, 41, 51, 58-59, 87, 93-95, 99-103, 108-10, 112, 115, 117, 120

Decision-making skills within OSRP, 4, 63-65, 67
Deficiencies, 1-2, 53-56, 65, 67, 69-71, 74, 77, 79-80, 84, 105, 107-108, 110, 113, 120

Field trips, 19, 23-24, 29-30, 47
Fine, Michelle, 2, 109, 117, 120
Freire, Paulo, 8-9

Gender barriers to mobility, 39-40, 47, 51, 57, 61, 109-10, 112
Gerald, 10, 16, 19-21, 23-24, 26-28, 30-32, 35, 37, 42-45, 48-50, 54-61, 63, 65-67, 69-70, 78-80, 99-100, 124
Giroux, Henry, 111, 120
Gouldner, Alvin W., 8
Grades: of OSRP students, 22-24, 32; perceptions of by parents, 21, 76; by students, 23, 40-41, 73, 76; by staff, 24, 66

Ideology, 7-8, 12-13, 36, 40-42, 44-51, 65, 74, 106, 109, 111-12, 114-16. *See also* Conservative Ideology of Hope
Implications, 117-19
Institutional caring, 108, 118

Jane, 15-16, 37, 43-44, 49-50, 54-59, 62-63, 65-66, 69-71, 77-79, 100-01
Job-trailing: employer-employee relations, 16-17, 19, 23-27, 30-31, 65, 115, 123-24

About the Author

BRAM A. HAMOVITCH is an assistant professor in the Department of Foundations of Education at Youngstown State University, Youngstown, Ohio. He has published articles on various aspects of the sociology of education in *Educational Foundations* and *Urban Education*.

ISBN 0-275-95701-2

90000>

HARDCOVER BAR CODE